NAMING

LAGUNA BEACH

by Jane Janz

Published by Pacific-Noir Press

Copyright © 2018 by Jane Janz

All rights reserved. No part of this publication may be reproduced, stored in a retrieval system, or transmitted, in any form or by any means, electronic, mechanical, photocopying, recording, or otherwise, without the prior written permission of the author.

ISBN-13: 978-0-9849504-4-7

Printed in the United States of America

Text by Jane Janz
Edited by Criag Lockwood
Design and Typography by Michael McCullen

Pacific-Noir Press
www.Pacific-Noir.com
1278 Glenneyre St.
Laguna Beach, CA 92651

DEDICATION

This is dedicated to all the past and present residents of Laguna Beach. Every single person who lived here influenced the town of Laguna in one way or another. Each was painting a piece of the canvas. Some used wide brushes and painted largely. Others used smaller brushes contributing in varying degrees. Add in the artists who had an eye for the breathtaking beauty. Pencil in the writers who were able to put into words how they felt about this special place.

But mostly there were just townspeople who lived, worked and raised their families here and worked very hard to establish schools, and joined service organizations without which this town would never have been able to function. Each and every one of them contributed to the Laguna of today, the only thing that varied was the size of their brush.

Table Of Contents

Introduction: It All Started With A Copper Teapot 7

Part One: Laguna Beach And How It Got Its Name 13

Laguna Beach 22

Arch Beach 26

Aliso 27

Part Two: The Post Office Story 29

Arch Beach 30

Lagona Beach 32

Lagona 37

Finally, Laguna Beach 40

Nick Isch's Store And Post Office 42

Four Families 49

Florence Yoch 61

Getting The Mail Into Town
  "Neither Snow, Nor Rain, Nor Heat..." 63

Changing Postmasters 72

Biggest Rush 80

Set In Stone 93

South Laguna 113

Some Who Served 122

Sources: Books 124

INTRODUCTION

IT ALL STARTED WITH A COPPER TEAPOT

It was about 1940 and I was taken by the hand and walked across the street from my grandparent's house to a small stucco building that housed a treasure trove of adventure and imagination. Walking in the door I knew instinctively that this place was filled with things I wanted to know. The Laguna Beach Library would be a source of many hours of exploration into the fascinating unknown.

My first library card had a small metal rectangle up in the corner that held the numbers that allowed me to check out books. I recall the exact sound that was made when that card was inserted by the librarian, Mrs. Case, into the checkout machine. It had a distinctive ker-chunk sound to it. It was sheer joy to pull out a drawer of the card catalogue, and there each and every book was listed on its own card. There was a children's section with oak chairs and a round table that were my size. I stood wide-eyed at the sight of all those books. I looked up at the shelves, and decided then and there that I would read every book in the children's section, start-

Laguna Beach Branch Library
363 Glenneyre

ing with those under A. I do remember "Johnny Appleseed," and then I got to "Astronomy." That was my un-doing, I never made it to the B section.

Years later I was researching a former copper business operating in Laguna in the past. They had made a copper teapot marked "Craftsman Studios Hand Made Laguna Beach, Calif." that I bought at an estate sale. I started calling some of the old-timers I had known for years, hoping they could tell me of this company and who started it. However, while information about Craftsman Studios was sparse, these wonderful people knew that I was also a local, and descended from old-timers, and they instinctively knew I would love to hear their stories of "you-know-who-and-who-did-what." I listened, knowing that I was hearing of the many small acts that are the ingredients of the story of how this town became the way it is.

Somewhere along the way in my quest for copper information, I was told that the old Laguna Beach newspapers were on microfilm down at the Laguna Library and perhaps I would find my answers there. So in 1993 once again I crossed the threshold of the library, into the world of adventure.

Gone was the cozy stucco building, gone were the card catalogues I loved to rifle through. And forever changed was how you learn - now you faced a screen instead of turning pages. The perfectly sized chair was gone—replaced with an uncomfortable stool that was just the wrong height for comfort, where you precariously perched in front of an instrument of torture - the microfilm reader. The monster reading machine screen sat at a strange angle, requiring a bend of the neck to see the screen as you tried to move the film up and down and back and forth with the controls. The result was after about one hour you had a gigantic headache from the monster machine. I often said, not jokingly, that to learn Laguna history you had to take two aspirin and go to the library. Fortunately, those machines are long gone.

In my first ten minutes of using that machine, I gasped as I read in wonder, and I admit to a tear or two. Here were the names I had heard growing up. Just names, I didn't really know the details about these people. But here they were. Who they were and what they did was there for the reading. There were reports about the early days of lack of water, how the locals fought to keep cheap amusements out of town, stories of artists I had known as a child. And most moving of all was an ad placed in that paper by my grandfather, Nick Isch, about items he was selling at his combination General Store and Post Office. At that moment my fate was sealed. I was started down the path of discovery with an interest that evolved into trying to find all I could about Laguna Beach and how it became the way it is. This time I did make it all the way through the alphabet, to the Zs.

And it all started with a copper teapot.

For years I have been asked: "When are you going to write a book?" My honest answer always has been that I don't know enough. I still don't. And writing a book has never been my goal. But after years of gathering information I realized the need to compile some of what I have learned.

This first endeavor starts with how the town was named and the important role played by the Post Office in that story. Laguna Beach is a unique place, first blessed with natural beauty, and secondly blessed with all who have directed her along the path that leads us to the Laguna of today.

And that small stucco library building building where this all began - it still exists. Years ago it was moved out into Laguna Canyon and became a private residence. I drove by it not long ago and my mind flashed back to those early experiences as I fondly remembered what it was like to walk through its door.

— Jane Petty Janz

FIRST TIME CANADA DE LAS LAGUNAS WAS USED

The map showing Canada de las lagunas was the genesis for how Laguna Beach was named. Is it known who first put that name on that map?

Orange County historian Phil Brigandi responded to that question.

"The rancho map is most likely the first time the Laguna name appears on a map. Unfortunately, it is difficult to date or know who drew it. It was drawn to show Jose Sepulveda's Rancho San Joaquin - later the southern end of the Irvine Ranch.

But the name was surely given by the mission fathers. The earliest I have found it in the mission records is in 1827, when the missionaries at San Juan Capistrano report that, "In the Laguna and in the Cienega, which are on the road from this Mission to the said estancia of Santa Ana, the herds water as also in the river of the same name."

The full report can be found in Fr. Zephyrin Engelhardt's Mission San Juan Capistrano, (1922) pp 86-94 Standard Printing Co. Los Angeles

PART ONE

LAGUNA BEACH AND HOW IT GOT ITS NAME

Laguna Beach town was born of different stock than the rest of Orange County, and from the beginning its growth-patterns were not like those of the area around it. The town would continue, through its entire history, to follow a path different from neighboring communities and other beach towns.

Geographically it was blessed with what world travelers would call one of the most beautiful shorelines in the world. Behind that coastline were hills that gave the town a feeling of being `enclosed. Over centuries the rain rushed from those hills to the sea which in the process broke up the flatness of the narrow strip of land and carved several large canyons and smaller picturesque gullies which added to the beauty.

Another geologic wonder was Laguna Canyon, the only way into the town. Early travelers frequently referred with awe to its natural beauty and the exhilaration and wonder they felt when they saw the canyon walls, the rock outcroppings and the stream and trees. Approaching Big Bend they were sure they had taken a wrong turn because it appeared to be a dead end. Suddenly they reached the end of the winding road and steep cliffs and had the beach spread out before them.

How this piece of empty treeless land, with no buildings, roads, or people would evolve into this unique town is the story of countless contributions and decisions made by each and every person who ever lived here.

What follows, the post office story, is a good place to start, because it provides us with some of the earliest documented records for the town, and helps explain some of the beginnings of a very long story of why Laguna Beach is as it is, today.

The first detail that sets Laguna apart from the development of the surrounding county. *It was not part of one of the large Ranchos formed from the Spanish and Mexican Land Grants.*

California, first colonized as part of Spain, and later as part of Mexico, was comprised primarily of very large parcels of land that had been granted under that system. A Spanish land grant was first bequeathed in 1784, and after that the land grants from Mexico started in 1824.[1]

These huge parcels of land in what would become Orange County were used primarily for the raising of cattle. To establish boundaries for these holdings surveys were done, which consisted of two men on horseback measuring off the land with a length of rope. "*Corner posts on a grant were sometimes branded with the owner's iron, or cattle mark; but often the most convenient objects at hand – a steer's skull fixed in a bush, a clump of cactus, a few notches on a tree-trunk, the place where two roads crossed, a mound at the entrance to a coyote's den, the edge of a dry barranca, a brush ramada on the banks of a stream, a spring of running water – were made to serve as boundary marks. With the passage of the years such landmarks usually*

---

1. Robert Glass Cleland, "From Wilderness to Empire" p. 129

disappeared or became almost impossible to locate and identify."[2] Occasionally there were spaces between Ranchos that were not claimed. These areas were called *"no grant"* land.

For some reason the area that would later become Laguna Beach was one of the larger pieces that was not part of any of those surrounding ranchos. This triangle of land had been left off the maps. There have been different reasons offered for this omission, but nothing that can be documented that I have been able to find. Was it because a family was already living near the entrance to the canyon? Or the surrounding hills that made it unsuitable for cattle grazing? There is the possibility that one rancho simply didn't realize that the neighboring rancho hadn't claimed it – a surveying slip up. One can only speculate what was in the minds of those early grantees.

California would become part of the United States with the passing of the Treaty of Guadalupe Hidalgo, in 1848. Even then it was impossible to buy land in this small triangle because it was government property.

The American government commissioned surveys of the new public lands and 1855 marked the beginnings of surveys for this area. In 1875, one surveyor noted in his field notes the following observations:

"The land in this township produces but very little vegetation of any value and what little feed there is grows so high up among the rocks that it is almost out of the reach of stock. The water of Laguna Creek is quite salty. The ground rises half a mile from the ocean level to about 1,000 feet. There are a few sycamore trees in the canon, but the timber is chiefly Elder and Willow. There is a pleasant place on the beach at the mouth of this canon and it is quite a resort."[3]

2. Cleland, "From Wilderness.." p. 132
3. City of Laguna Beach. "Guidelines for Shoreline Protection." April 1, 1988

The United States Government wanted to get their land into private hands so that it could be developed. To do that they passed laws that would allow that to happen, thus the Homestead Acts, which led to settlement across this huge continent.

The attempts to pass Homestead Acts had been tried before but were blocked because the southern states wanted the western lands open for settlement by slave-owners.[4] The southern states also feared that their work force would leave to go and claim land of their own.

Civil War broke out and the South seceded, enabling the federal government to pass The Homestead Act of 1862, signed into law by President Abraham Lincoln. The Homestead Act was in effect from 1863 to 1908.

In general, this gave an applicant ownership of 160 acres of land by following a few steps. A person wishing to go through the process of acquiring homestead land this way was called an "entryman" and filed what were called "land entry" papers and each case was assigned a case number. After filing for it, the applicant had to improve the land, build a structure of 12 x 14, grow crops, and live on the land for five years. "Title could also be acquired after only a 6-month residency and trivial improvements, provided the claimant paid the government $1.25 per acre. After the Civil War, Union soldiers could deduct the time they had served from the residency requirements."[5] Requirements met, the owner would pay a small fee and get a patent of ownership.

Of course there were countless attempts at abuse of these laws all across the country, though none here locally that I know of. An example of this is the dispute over whether the law meant a dwelling had to be 12 by 14 feet, or 12 by

---

4. Wikipedia. Homestead Acts - background.
5. www.ourdocuments.gov

14 inches.[6] Another enterprising homesteader built a house on a carriage and moved the carriage-house to a number of different homesteads he had claimed, astutely taking photographs of all the homes he had built to prove up the land.

Later, Congress passed the Timber Culture Act of 1873. When this law was first enacted the government offered 160 acres if 40 acres were planted with trees. The Act was amended a number of times, which included a change in the number of acres that had to be planted to trees. Due to such fraudulent use of the Timber Culture Act it was repealed in 1891 after being in existence only 18 years.[7]

Also remember that some of these homesteads changed hands several times before the final patent was signed, so that the name of the homestead patent holder was not necessarily the same name as that of the "entryman." Buying and selling was going on from the very beginning. This difference in entryman and patent (owner) names often leads to difficulties in determining just *who* planted *which* group of trees, or built *which* building.

Due to the original-source research done by Beryl Viebeck we now have a list and a beautiful map showing all the homesteads granted in this triangle of land. Viebeck's information includes who was granted the patent, and the date that occurred. From it we find that over these three sections of land that comprise the Laguna Beach of today there were a **total of 39 homesteads, held by 37 different people.**

This map clearly shows the *three townships*, Laguna Beach, Arch Beach, and Aliso were delineated by diagonal lines drawn across the original triangle. Suprisingly, these designations show that Arch Beach was a term used for the

---

6. www.ourdocuments.gov from the National Archives, Wash. D.C. "Homestead Act of 1862."
7. MNOPEDIA. "The Timber Culture Act of 1873.

PART OF LAGUNA ROAD DISTRICT

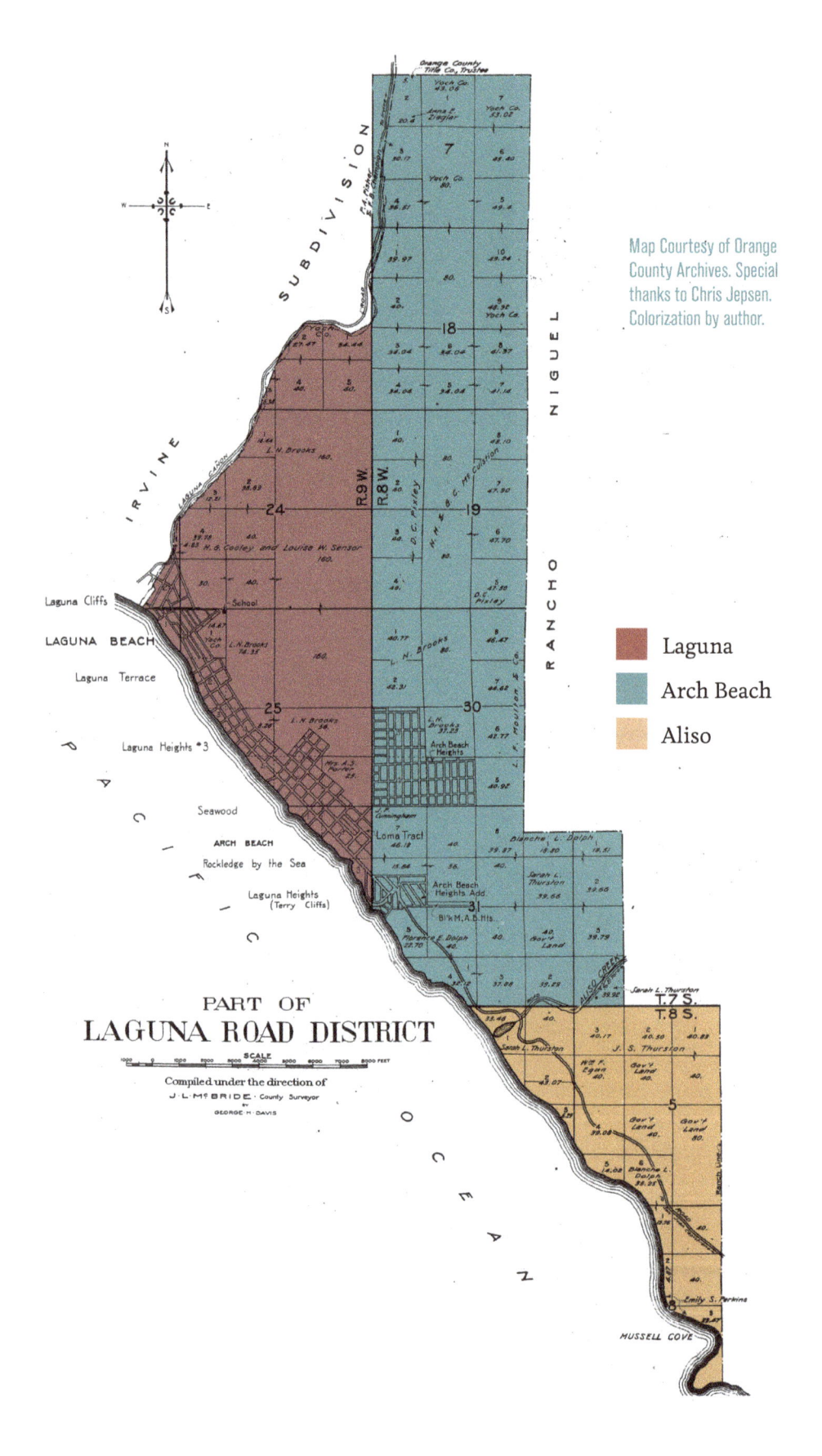

Compiled under the direction of
J. L. McBRIDE, County Surveyor
by
GEORGE H. DAVIS

Map Courtesy of Orange County Archives. Special thanks to Chris Jepsen. Colorization by author.

- Laguna
- Arch Beach
- Aliso

early homesteads way out in Laguna Canyon, across the hills, down to the beach. The actual Arch Beach ocean frontage only ran from Victoria Beach South to about Westley Dr.

Over the years these names would be used in different ways to describe different areas, which has caused confusion. As the town became subdivided and the population grew, in usage these same three names evolved into names for land that implied slightly different areas.

Arch Beach in particular has had its borders shifted over periods of time. First, the name was applied to the large homestead-period township. Secondly, it was used for the small town of Arch Beach whose name appears on lists of failed towns due to the real estate collapse of the 1880s. This area centered around the Diamond Street area. Thirdly, and for the largest period of time, the name of Arch Beach was applied to approximately Sleepy Hollow, on south to Nyes Place.

Early newspapers made a very clear distinction between the two towns of Laguna Beach and Arch Beach. Often in the local papers there appeared lists of current buildings under construction, and these usually would say if the residence under construction was in Arch Beach or Laguna. Residents who lived in Arch Beach often spoke of *"going over to Laguna."*

Officially Arch Beach was made part of Laguna with incorporation in 1927. But the distinction continued on, with newspaper articles still making use of the name of Arch Beach. Even as late as 1931, it was stated that the new Catholic Church built on Temple Terrace was being built in Arch Beach.

To add to the confusion, many old photos and postcards of the area are titled *"Arch Beach."* There is no one beach named Arch Beach—the photos are referring to the separate area of Arch Beach.

The Homestead Act was designed to allow people to settle on and farm the land. In Laguna, farming was difficult, so once again Laguna took a different tack.

A large part of many of these ocean-oriented homesteads were comprised of steep slopes, hills and canyons. And there was no available water. Farming did occur in some sections of Laguna, but considering the total number of acres involved in the homesteads, that was rare.

What early homesteaders did recognize was that the moderate temperature and natural beauty of the coast, seashore, and backdrop of beautiful hills was their greatest asset. Even before homesteading-ownership occurred, people had come to Laguna to camp in the summertime to escape the high heats of inland areas. No town in Orange County could claim as beautiful an entrance as Laguna Canyon, for years the only way into town. In Laguna the primary chance to make an income from the land was to subdivide it into buildable lots and to lure people here to buy those lots.

© Copyrighted by Beryl Viebeck and printed with permission given by her daughter Carol Lloyd

JANE JANZ

LAGUNA BEACH

On early maps of the triangular piece of land that later would be called Laguna Beach, there were no identifying names other than Aliso Creek. However, north of that near the Rancho San Joaquin, there were two lakes that are located in the Canada de Las Lagunas, today's Laguna Canyon. This name appears on a map dated as early as 1841.[8]

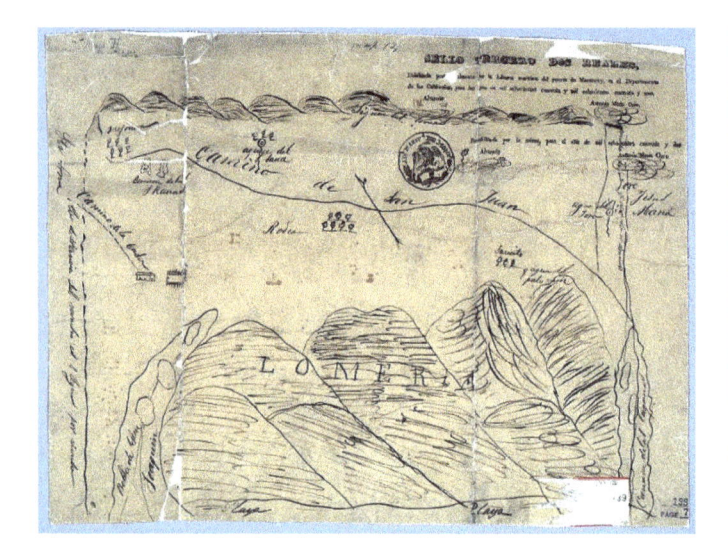

Edwin Gudde In *"California Place Names"* says of the word Laguna *"The Spanish geographical term designates generally a small lake."* He then continues to list the different usages used on those early maps up and down the state of California. It was used for large lakes, and even shallow marshy Tulare Lake was originally called Laguna de Tache. There are Laguna Points, Arroyos, Peaks and Creeks, Saladas,

Photo Credit: Orange County Archives. Provided by Chris Jepsen.

---

8. "The Dictionary of California Land Names" compiled by Phil Townsend Hanna. Automobile Club of Southern California, Los Angeles, 1946. P. 148

Namesake lake in the canyon.
Credit: LB Historical Society.

Hondas, Secas and Zecas, to name only a few. *"The name Laguna appears in the titles of more than thirty land grants and claims"*[9] up, down and around the state. *And none of those usages were in the acreage of what would become Laguna Beach.*

So the obvious question is what happened? The name travelled.

As people started coming down the Canyon of the Lagunas the name for that canyon became the identifying name. The Los Angeles Times newspaper started in 1881, and by 1882 the name Laguna appeared five times in that paper. One talks of "a camping trip to the beach at Laguna Canyon." Another states that "at Laguna Canyon there is fine surf, and good fishing." Obviously, the surf and fishing are not out in the canyon itself. One article is titled "Laguna Canyon - Life at the Seaside." That year, the town was referred to as Laguna Beach twice more, and The Laguna once. In 1883 the town is mentioned fourteen times. "Laguna cañon, one of the finest resorts on the coast…" stands out as a good example of name evolution in progress.

The names "Laguna canyon", "Laguna Beach", "The Laguna", "Laguna", and the "New Laguna Colony" were used. The numbers of articles using the name of Laguna contin-

9. "California Place Names" Edwin G. Gudde. University of California Press. Third Edition p.169

Laguna Canyon Road
Irvine ranch on right.
Credit: LB Historical Society.

ued to increase over the years ahead. One of the memorable quotes was "at Laguna there are tents, fish, and swells (two kinds)."[10]

To further establish that Laguna Beach is the historical name of the town the first subdivision maps from that time period can be used. The first and oldest map of down-town Laguna was surveyed by C.C. Miller in 1883, for Henry E. Goff for his homestead that included the area south of Park Ave. which included where Hotel Laguna stands today. That map was titled "Map of Laguna Beach."

It is interesting to note that from the very beginning the residents of Riverside played a hand in the development of the town. C.C. Miller, resident of Riverside, was the father of Frank Miller who bought his father's rooming house and

10. LA Times. Aug. 10, 1883

developed it into the famous Mission Inn. Frank Miller later built the beautiful Villa Rockledge in Laguna. Many Riverside residents had their eyes on Laguna Beach from the very beginning.

In 1887, S.H. Finley did maps for George Rogers who subdivided what now is the Forest Avenue area, and those maps also show the name Laguna Beach.

The basic street configuration on those maps has been retained over the years, and in many cases the names have been kept. Each subdivider chose the street names for their tract. There were repetitions (three Beach Streets) and it took years for all the confusion to be settled. Glenneyre is a good example—in different subdivisions it had different names that years later would be changed. Originally that name was used only in the most southerly part of Arch Beach while in other homesteads it had different names, including Central Avenue, First St. and Avenue R.

It should also be noted that because a street appeared on a map does not mean the street was ever graded or existed at that time. Another lasting result of those early subdivision maps was that their streets didn't always meet up with a street in a neighboring map, resulting in places like Glenneyre St. where it crosses Thalia St., which to this day requires a jog to maneuver.

ARCH BEACH

The naming of this area took a different route. Pioneer Joe Thurston said that neighboring homesteaders Hub Goff and Nate Brooks "went in together and started the town of Arch Beach (which takes its name from an arch that is formed by the rocks on the beach.)" [11]

A son of William Brooks wrote in a letter dated in 1966, that it was his mother, Annie Brooks, who named the area based on the arch in the rocks. [12] That arch is near the foot of Pearl Street.

The Los Angeles Times' first mention of the town of Arch Beach was not until 1887. It was also in 1887, that the first tract maps appear. The first is titled Arch Beach Plat 1 "being situated on land belonging to L.N. Brooks, H.S. Goff, and Harry E. Stafford." This covered the area from Bluebird Canyon Drive south to Upland.

A note about the name Goff – there were four Goff brothers. There has been some confusion due to the fact that two of them were named H.Goff. H.S. (Hubbard) is the one who homesteaded in the southern part of town and started the Arch Beach Hotel. H.E. (Henry) subdivided the area just south of Park Ave., in the area where Hotel Laguna is found.

The second map, also filed in 1887, is a tract map titled Plat ll Map of A Part of Arch Beach. This shows the area from Cleo Street south to Calliope Street, and though his name does not appear on the map, the land was owned by Nate Brooks.

---

11. "Laguna Beach of Early Days" J.S. Thurston. p.50-51
12. Letter from Clarence H. Brooks, Aug. 17, 1966. Author's copy.

ALISO

The third Homestead section, Aliso, started at about Wesley Dr. and ran all the way to the southern end of today's Three Arch Bay. It was the last section to become populated and had sections that were devoted to farming. It included the Thurston Ranch in Aliso Canyon.

Aliso Canyon

What would become South Laguna later. About 1st. Ave.
Credit: Laguna Beach Library Karen Turnbull Collection

So, we have the original names of the towns established and the origin of how those names evolved and came into being.

But then a horrible thing happened.

The name of Laguna Beach was gone, taken away, lost forever.

It happened on May 15, 1891.

The identity, name and address for this lovely village was destined never to be the same, never to be Laguna Beach. To learn how this could happen we need to look into Post Office history.

PART TWO

THE POST OFFICE STORY

The following dates used concerning postmasters and locations were taken directly from the records kept in the National Archives. Also, to better understand their policies, it is best to examine a direct quote about how they were chosen. "*From 1836 to 1971, postmasters at the larger Post Offices were appointed by the President, by and with the consent of the Senate. Postmasters earning less than $1,000 per year were appointed by the Postmaster General, generally upon the advice of the local congressman or townspeople.*

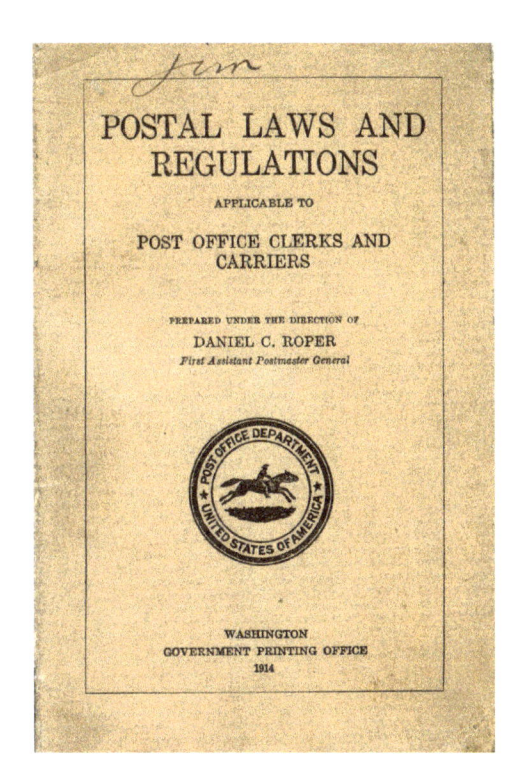

Regulations required that postmasters execute a valid bond and take an oath of office. Since 1971, postmasters have been selected through the merit system. Women have served as postmasters since the Revolutionary War and even earlier, under British rule. 'Postmaster,' and not 'Postmistress,' always has been their official title."[13]

13. USPS FAQs about Postmaster Finder

JANE JANZ

ARCH BEACH

Arch Beach, that large section of land, and separate town, that ran from about Cleo St. on south approximately to Nyes Place became home to the first post office to be established in the area. That year, 1889, coincided with the formation of Orange County which had recently been carved out of Los Angeles County. It was also the year after Southern California experienced a huge real estate market collapse which was the result of extensive wild speculation. That collapse in property prices would have grave consequences for the early homesteaders of Laguna and would also have an effect on the progression of the community's post offices.

Oliver N. Brooks was the first postmaster and the date for Laguna's first post office was June 21, 1889. He was postmaster for only four months. Oliver N. Brooks, had been the lighthouse keeper of Faulkners Light off the coast of Connecticut for 31 years, where he lived with his wife and twelve children. He came to Arch Beach in 1887, and started working with Hubbard Goff who was building a hotel at the foot of Diamond Street, which Goff called the "Arch Beach House." By 1890, Brooks was back in Connecticut. It should be pointed out that this is *not* Oliver S. Brooks, brother of Will and Nate Brooks.[14]

Oliver N. Brooks, first PM at Arch Beach

14. Mark Whitman provided information on the correct Oliver Brooks and photo.

Arch Beach PO document

On Oct. 9, 1889, the Arch Beach postmaster became William Schkomodau, or Schkomdau, both spellings were used. His tenancy was for two years. Mrs. Lulu Stocking, one of the Hubbard Goff daughters, became postmaster on Nov. 25, 1891. One year later Chas. D. Ambrose took over on Nov. 2, 1892. He was the final postmaster in Arch Beach. That post office was closed on May 26, 1894, only five years after it opened. It was never reinstated.

LAGONA BEACH

Two years after the founding of a post office at Arch Beach, on May 15, 1891, a post office was opened in the separate town of Laguna Beach with William Brooks as the postmaster. That date was memorable in the history of Laguna Beach, because it marks the end of the established and documented name of Laguna Beach. The name from then on would become of all things LAGONA BEACH.

How did this happen? It had nothing to do with a name mix-up with Long Beach. It had nothing to do with ancient Indian names, which was a myth passed down for years.

In fact in 1964, a group of Laguna residents, hoping to find if the myth was true or not, went down to San Juan Capistrano and contacted descendants of the early Indians in that area. Antonio Oliveras stated that he had never heard of the word Laguna, Lagona or any similar name used in their language, nor one that even resembled that word.[15] In fact there is only one name in Orange County that is derived from an Indian name and that is Niguel.[16]

The word 'laguna' is definitely of Spanish origin, so the name Lagona wasn't a typographical error, and certainly the irate Laguna residents had nothing to do with it. Instead it had everything to do with the United States Post Office Department.

A copy of the original form "Post Office Site Location" signed by William Brooks in April of 1891, documents this claim. These forms were provided by the Postmaster General and were to be filled out by anyone seeking establishment of a post office, or when there was a proposed change in postmaster. The handwriting giving all the necessary informa-

---

15. South Coast News. July 1964
16. Orange County Place Names A to Z. by Phil Brigandi.

tion required shows the name of *Laguna* (with a "u") *Beach* in three different places. *Yet, when the request was granted, across the top of the filled-out form, the Post Office Department had boldly written Lagona Beach.* A puzzlement indeed.

To explain this requires going back to California's original Ranchos. **Throughout California the name "Laguna" was used in over thirty different Spanish and Mexican land grants.** That, of and by itself, created considerable competition for the use of the name. It took a lot of searching, checking, and comparing of dates for different post offices to finally find the solution. The answer was found in *"A Century of California Post Offices"* by Walter N. Frickstad. By making lists containing the name Laguna, and then checking dates for their post offices, the puzzle was solved. **In San Diego County a post office was established there on June 17, 1889, and was called Laguna, California. That explains why the historic name of Laguna Beach ceased to exist. As far as the Post Office Department was concerned the name Laguna was already taken.**

A perfect example of life's ironies is that on Oct. 10, 1891, that same Laguna, San Diego County post office went out of existence. If William Brooks had applied after Oct. 10, 1891 instead of in April of 1891, the outcome would have been completely different.

Laguna however wasn't the only town in the area to lose its name. Irvine also did not receive their original request for post office name. They received a Post Office on May 20, 1899, and of course had applied for the name of Irvine.

Washington wouldn't allow it. There was already a town in Calaveras County named Irvine. Thus Irvine became "*Myford,*" named for James Irvine's year-old son. It wasn't until 1914 that their historic name was reinstated when the northern town changed their name to "Carson Hill."[17]

Where the Lagona Beach Post Office was housed in 1891, is unknown. Period post office site location forms didn't require exact addresses, locations, or building names.

In 1887, Kate and Joe Yoch moved from Illinois to Santa Ana following the sale of the Yoch Brothers coal mines. They had many business interests in the area. Joseph Yoch was on the County Board of Supervisors from Jan. 5, 1891, until Jan. 7, 1895.

Pertinent to Laguna history, they purchased significant property in Laguna Beach including one of the first cottages on Main Beach. Joe and his fellow ocean-front cottage owners all pitched in building the first boardwalk in the sand in front of their cottages. It took one day.

In 1893 the Yochs financed the building of a new hotel in Laguna, the Brooks Hotel, with William Brooks managing.

This new hotel is not to be confused with any other hotel site, as it was built new, and was situated in the 300 block of what would eventually become the South Coast

Catherine and Joe Yoch, daughters Elizabeth, Josephine, Kate, Bertha

17. Gudde, Erwin G. "California Place Names." p. 153

1893 Brooks Hotel. Ocean Side-300 block S. Coast Blvd. Credit: LB Historical Society

Highway, approximately across the street from today's White House Restaurant, not on the site of the present Hotel Laguna.

The Brooks Hotel opened in May of 1893, and housed the *Lagona Beach Post Office*, with William Brooks the first post master in this part of town. Only four months later, on Sept. 11 of that same year, 1893, the hotel caught fire and was destroyed. The Yoch cottage on the boardwalk was singed during that fire which had started in, of all places, the Post Office. *That marks Sept. 11, 1893, as the end of the Lagona Beach Post Office, it ceased to exist.* William Brooks had been postmaster for two years. From then on, mail destined for Lagona Beach would be sent to the post office at Arch Beach, at that date run by Charles Ambrose. *As stated, that post office also went out of existence only one year later, in 1894.*

Just to clarify, there has been some confusion about the hotel fire over the years. It was the *Brooks Hotel* that burned down, *not* the Hotel Laguna. There were two reasons why the confusion arose. Joe and Kate Yoch owned both properties, and it took a long time and a lawsuit to collect the insurance money from the Brooks Hotel fire.

Newspaper articles talk about the Brooks Hotel fire, and there are articles about how long it took Yoch to collect the insurance on that hotel.

"Joseph Yoch vs. the Home Mutual Insurance Company, an action to recover on an insurance policy was filed Saturday with the County Clerk. This action refers to the policy that was issued on the Laguna Hotel which was destroyed by the fire about three months ago."[18] That article was written in January of 1894, four months after the Brooks Hotel fire.

"J. Yoch of Santa Ana has received the insurance money from the Home Mutual Insurance Company on account of the burning of the hotel at Laguna Beach about two years ago.... The insurance company at first refused to pay the loss, but Mr. Yoch took the case to the Supreme Court, and the claim was ordered paid. The amount was $4,976.25."[19] That was published in March 1896, three years after the loss of the Brook's Hotel. That insurance pay-out for the Brooks Hotel occurred *after* the Yochs had begun renovating the old abandoned hotel, just one block south of the burned hotel. In all probability over time people have seen the articles about the Laguna Hotel fire and have incorrectly assumed it was the hotel in the 400 block of North Coast Highway, today's Hotel Laguna.

In 1916, there was a flare-up fire in the kitchen of the hotel. It was quickly extinguished. The hotel itself did not burn.

---

18. Los Angeles Times. Jan. 7, 1894
19. Los Angeles Times. March, 1896

Boring Store and PO. Fred Trefren right rear with water barrells. Credit: LB Historical Society.

LAGONA

A new start was made in May of 1894, by Washington M. Boring who filled in the request for establishment of a Post Office in Laguna Beach. This time, the name Laguna appears twice in the form. When the appointment came back from the Post Office Department, on the top of that form, the government had entered the name Lagona Beach on the top part of that form, only this time they put several squiggly marks through the word Beach. The town now was reduced to one solitary meaningless word, Lagona.

Why had they removed "Beach?" In April 8, 1894, the Postmaster General issued order 114, which says

"To remove cause of annoyance to the Department and injury to the Postal Service in the selection of names for newly established post offices, it is herby ordered that from this date only short names or names of one word will be accepted. Names of post offices will be changed only for reasons satisfactory to the Department."

Boring document shows how Beach was lost

JANE JANZ

The Post Office Department wanted no usage of Corners, Peak, Town, Point, Center, Old, Hollow, Vale, or Beach, to name only a few. So the townspeople and visitors were stuck with a name that didn't match what they called the town, and they stubbornly went on calling it Laguna Beach anyway, even if there was no reason to think that the name would ever be reinstated. Joe and Kate Yoch continued printing their Hotel envelopes with *Laguna Beach* as its return address, even when the cancellation mark placed on that envelope when mailed said "Lagona." The author has personally seen a Rand McNally map that showed the town as "Lagona."

Lagona's post office had been housed in Boring's store for the one year he was postmaster.

Lagona 1898 postmark
Laguna Beach House Hotel

Kate and Joe Yoch and friend at Alpha Cottage on the boardwalk

Nick and Young Maurice Isch PO

In August of 1895, Boring's store was bought by Joseph Yoch and a new post office and store was built in front of it.[20] In August of 1895 Joseph Yoch was appointed postmaster of Lagona, California, even though his place of residence was Santa Ana.

As the Yoch's residence was in Santa Ana and they stayed here only part-time during the summer at their cottage on the boardwalk, it was John Nicholas Isch, his brother in law, who moved to Laguna and became assistant postmaster. He was the one who would be the person behind the counter and filling the boxes with mail.

Starting in 1895, for the next twenty-five years, it would be Nick Isch who was identified with the post office, in fact most people assumed he was postmaster from that time on. Even County Directories listed his occupation as postmaster. Nick Isch did become postmaster of Lagona on April 29, 1903.

20. South Coast News. Sept. 11, 1930

FINALLY, LAGUNA BEACH

It was postmaster Nick Isch, On Sept. 17, 1904, who brought about the change in the Post Office Department's decision to reinstate the town's historical and still used name of Laguna Beach. A little chronology is in order: until 1904, the policy had been to assign plain, simple single-word names. This policy was often undermined by local conditions, as in Laguna Beach where the locals went right on calling their home Laguna Beach, even if the government wouldn't.

Starting in 1904, the Post Office Department in Washington D.C. decided to give in to those concerns and agreed to accept variations. So Nick Isch convinced them that in usage the people of this small community called their town Laguna Beach, and the change was made.

Laguna's townspeople were overjoyed, grateful that the true name of the village was reinstated. When he died in 1951 they still referred to him as the man who was responsible for the town being named *Laguna Beach.*"

The days of frequent change in postmaster were over. For twenty five years it would be Nick Isch in the post office passing out the mail and watching every event, every visitor, and every person who contributed to Laguna Beach becoming what it was. If only he had written a book. It was this post office and store which became a legend. That store's existence coincided with a period in Laguna's history that many of the residents cherished and thought best represented Laguna at its most charming. This 1895-Yoch -sponsored attempt at the recovery from the financial disaster of 1888, which had marked the end of the homestead period, started the town back on a rich path of gentle, steady, picturesque growth.

Joseph Kleitsch
"The Old Post Office"
Credit: LB Art Museum

"Usually everything is dated from the Isch Grocery store period which was when history began for Laguna Beach."[21]

21. South Coast News, June 19, 1936

Isch PO
Credit: Beryl Viebeck

NICK ISCH'S STORE AND POST OFFICE

"We natives all remember how if you went down to Laguna after the vacation season was over you did not find any one in town except Mr. Nick Isch, who was postmaster and the only merchant. He was the same genial, kindly soul that he is today, and if you needed anything you went over to his store and bought or borrowed it, as the case might be, often the latter."[22]

To understand how it came into existence some background is necessary.

Henry Goff opened a rooming house in Laguna Beach in 1886, on the inland side of today's highway. He later added another cottage to the list of rentals. An early description of their physical location - "where the Villas are today" - means it was located about where the Glenneyre parking structure exists today. Goff sold his property and moved away from Laguna. A man named Spencer bought the build-

22. Mrs. J.E Pleasants. "History of Orange County, California" 1931

Spencer Hotel
Credit: LB Historical Society

ings and moved them to the ocean front and built the hotel that appears in old photos. Those early images showing the Hotel on the ocean front should more properly identify that building as "*Spencer Hotel.*"

California had a large influx of immigration starting in the 1860s which reached a fever pitch in the late 1880s. Because of wild land speculation the economy collapsed, coming to a halt in 1887-1888. Though Laguna was well removed from the boom's center, when the collapse occurred it had dire consequences on development of Laguna Beach. There were no buyers for the property and banks were not lending money.

Both hotels eventually failed, bankruptcy was declared and the buildings were abandoned, sitting empty and unused for many years. A history of the great real estate "boom" of Southern California, states that 1889 was *"the dullest year in business in real estate known for years."*[23] Riverside was among the few Southern California cities to survive, primarily because they were involved in developing their agriculture business rather than in land speculation that doomed other

---

23. Van Dyke, Theodore "Millionaires of a Day."

communities. Early Laguna and Arch Beach homesteaders had no buyers for their land and most just packed up and left. As years passed the two towns would lay dormant.

Joe and Kate Yoch had made one attempt at reviving the town, by building a hotel in Laguna in 1893, only to see it burn down only a few months later. So they then turned to the old abandoned empty Spencer Hotel building and started what is certainly the first major remodel job in Laguna Beach history. In 1895, it was fresh and ready for guests. It opened as the Laguna Beach Hotel. To accommodate people making the trip to Laguna and the "new" hotel, the Yochs sponsored a combination store - post office, and the Isch-Warling Livery Stable. They asked Nick Isch to move to Laguna, become assistant postmaster and to run the businesses. The Yochs bought a lot of property in Laguna and in the Canyon and began the long task of developing the town. *"For many years Mr.Yoch was the sole financial backer of the town."*[24]

From the earliest known photographs taken in the 1880s, you can see that the business part of town started up by the intersection of appropriately named Laguna Avenue and Coast Highway, at that time on the maps called Riverside Ave.

Forest Avenue was still exactly that, a forest. The home of George Rogers which was on Third Street near the entrance to the canyon was the only structure down in the flat part of the town. Everything north of the creek, which ran between what is today Broadway and Ocean Ave., was the Irvine Ranch.

In summertime campers would pitch their tents all along the shore front. In wintertime it was empty. There was no electricity, no gas, no water. Rain water was stored and collected in cisterns. There were a few scattered houses,

Opposite Page: Nick Isch creating a garden at Yoch Hotel (far left).1896, before Arch Beach Hotel added. White cottage at center is southernmost boardwalk cottage.

24. South Coast News. Jan. 15,1926

NAMING LAGUNA BEACH

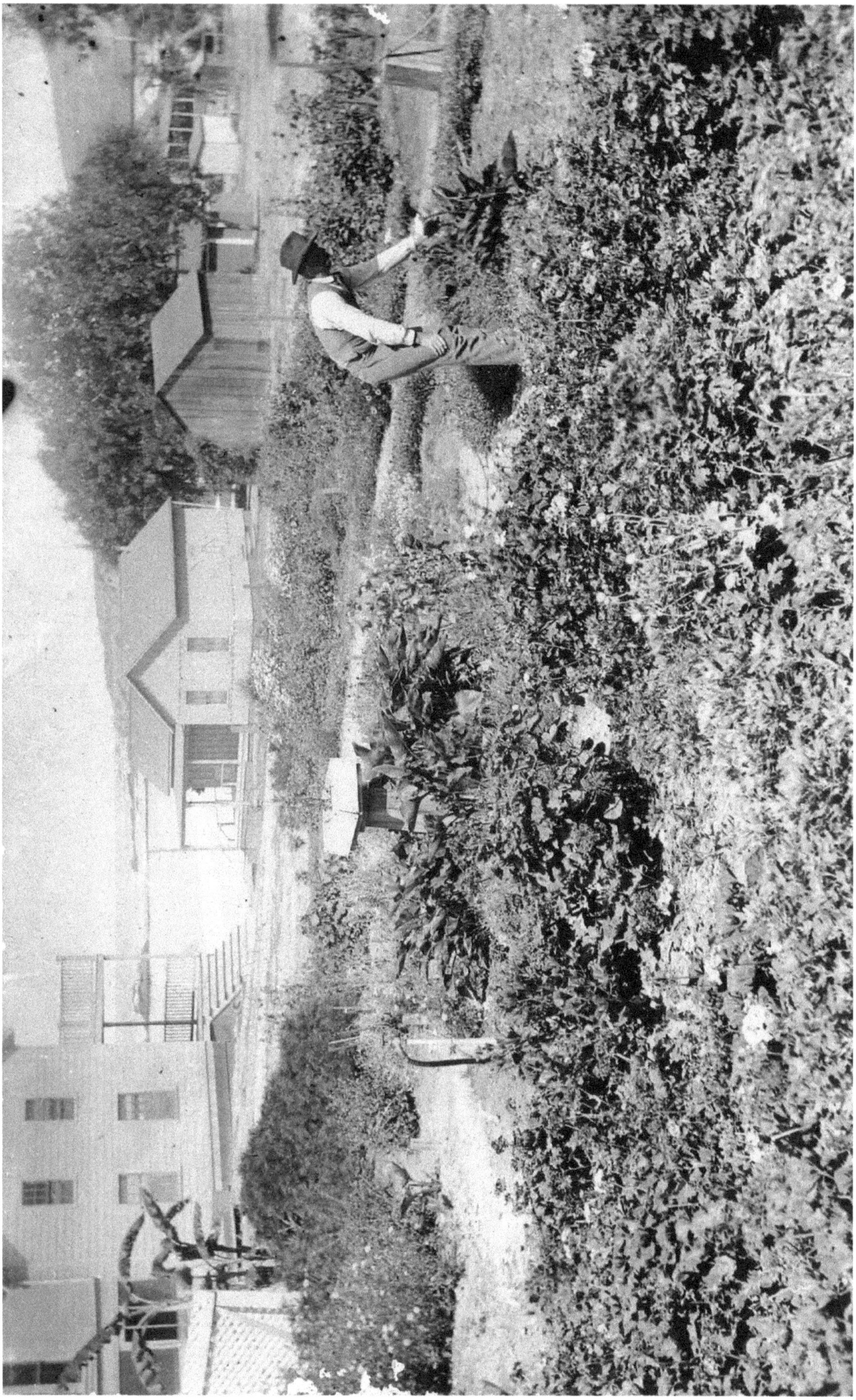

Stage arriving at Isch Store/PO

and most of those were occupied only in the summer. There were only three businesses in town, the Store -Post Office, the Isch- Warling Livery Stable, and the Hotel, and that was open only in the summer.

When the stage coaches arrived in Laguna they stopped at the store to make deliveries of goods and people. Anyone living in the area walked or rode horses to the store, tied up at the hitching post and sat on the porch to wait for the mail to be sorted. That porch became the social hub of the town and provided a sense of community. Real estate deals were made, gossip was passed, decisions were made, fights were fought, and most of all it was where people came to talk and get the latest news. It became a treasured memory in the minds of anyone coming to Laguna.

Poems were written about it, children wrote about their memories of it years later when they were adults, and it appeared in paintings. Every artist, writer, traveler or resident in the town walked up those stairs and knew that front porch. There was a place to tack notices. The door was usually open.

The famous Joseph Kleitsch painting "The Old Post Office" shows the view across the front steps of the old building.

PO, Nick Isch far right

Laguna's first documented fire-fighting equipment consisted of "a barrel of water and a dozen buckets, strung on a wooden arm."[25] These were at the old post office.

"Nick Isch was the postmaster, the storekeeper, the sage, the friend of everybody. It was in the spirit of service that he supplied the barrel and the buckets. From time to time the buckets were borrowed and never returned and there were times when the equipment had dwindled to a few pails."[26]

Mrs. Walter Joyce, (then Margaret Isch) told about one of the ocean-front boardwalk cottages that burned down. (The site was where the Las Ondas Café later was built.) The villagers grabbed the buckets and formed a bucket brigade from the ocean but it was not enough to save the cottage.[27]

Mrs. Joyce Brown Clark recalled that *"Mr. Isch's store was an oasis for us all. You tied up at the hitching post. They had everything from the latest news, our mail, kerosene for the lamps, groceries and yardage and sewing materials."*[28]

25. South Coast News. June 12, 1931.
26. South Coast News. Jan. 12, 1931
27. South Coast Nes. Jan. 12, 1931
28. South Coast News. March, 1955

M.F.K. Fisher, the famous food writer, in one of her books, recalled that as a child when her family, the Kennedys, used their summer cottage out in Arch Beach she remembered making trips to the Isch store for groceries, and they would stop to check the tide table that was tacked to the front door of the little hotel.[29] That cottage, owned by her parents, the Kennedy family of Whittier, was used in the summertime for over twenty-five years, and still exists, though remodeled, at 1370 Glenneyre Street.

29. MFK Fisher, "To Begin Again" p.29

FOUR FAMILIES

Years passed and the town grew, though slowly. Gavy Cravath, the famous baseball player, said that on his first trip to Laguna in 1900 *"The only permanent residents at that time were the four families of Nick Isch, Oscar Farman, Nate Brooks and Nate Philbrook."*[30] Out in the next town south, Arch Beach, Nate Brooks was dry farming south of Sleepy Hollow, and there were a few houses in Arch Beach none of which were occupied in the winter months. Gavy went on to say *"Oscar Farman's father, Fernando Farman, ran the stage. Mail came in twice a week. Those were big days at Nick Isch's post office. It usually amounted to three letters and several papers."*[31]

Nathan Philbrook, one of the four families mentioned, is a name that should be considered primary among the names of the earliest residents, businessmen, and contributors to the shaping of early Laguna Beach. Buying land in Laguna in 1887, he built his home and business on Forest Ave., the first to do so.[32] A brick layer and mason by trade, he dealt in real estate, was on the school board, and was elected Justice of the Peace.

One photo shows the house with Nate in his buggy and his wife sitting in a chair. He then added onto that house a white building slightly in front of the home. To clarify where it was situated his home clearly shows in the center of the photograph, right at the bend of the highway, on the corner of Forest Ave. and what would become the highway. As you are looking north down the highway, that is the White House Restaurant on the right in this photo.

30. South Coast News. Sept 18, 1944
31. South Coast News. Sept. 18, 1944
32. Santa Ana Register. July 30, 1909

Nate and Gertie Philbrook,
Forest Ave. about 1887
Philbrook Photos
Credit: Don Estep

N. PHILBROOK.
Real Estate.

Who built a cottage in Laguna Beach in 1887.

Agent for the Royal and Queen Insurance Co's. It required over $9000000.00 to settle their losses in the San Francisco fire which they paid without one cent discount.

Where the scenery is
          simply great
I conduct my business
          Real Estate.
Lots I have to sell.
Acreage, of course, as well.
Laguna Beach is where
          I dwell.
Ask for Uncle Phill;
They know me well.
N. PHILBROOK.
Notary Public.

Gertrude and Nate Philbrook and friends

Nate Philbrook home and office, just above name of Laguna Beach

JANE JANZ

Nate Brooks, Catherine Brooks, Guy Skidmore, Lee Skidmore and friend. Ocean front

Nate Brooks, an early homesteader and one of the few to stay after the financial collapse, lived in Arch Beach near the area of Bluebird Canyon where he did farming. In 1900, he moved his two-story house to the ocean front in Laguna after he married widow Catherine Skidmore who had four children. Nate died in 1914, and Catherine and her two sons took over management and development of his property.

Fernando Farman and his wife lived at one time in the old Rogers Ranch house. He moved to Laguna in 1892 and was the first to run the mail stage from El Toro to Laguna. He had one child, Oscar Farman. Oscar would eventually

Fernando Farman at El Toro train station

marry one of the Skidmore daughters, Lee. They had one child, Thelma Farman, who was born in the old Nate Brooks house, but was raised in Los Angeles and appeared in several silent movies. In 1918, Oscar, Lee and Thelma moved back to Laguna.

Nick Isch, with pole, Fred and Mrs. Mansur, children Mildred and Mabel Mansur. at Crescent Bay

John Nicholas Isch was born in Illinois where one of his sisters, Catherine Isch, married Joseph Yoch. The Yochs moved to Santa Ana in 1887. Nick Isch came to visit his sister in 1888, and was in Laguna for one year, then returned to his store in Illinois. He made the permanent move back to Laguna in 1895 becoming a local merchant and postmaster.

Kathryne Barnett was born and raised in Potsdam, New York. She became a school teacher and in 1893, she and three other adventurous teachers from Potsdam boarded a train and took off to pioneer in emerging California, on the way stopping in Chicago to attend the World's Fair.

Kathryne became a teacher in Ocean View, near present day Huntington Beach. She continued teaching there until her marriage to Nick Isch in 1898. She then taught at the Laguna school when it was situated near Canyon Acres. There

KATHRYNE ISCH ON ROCK, MRS. MANSUR

were not enough students to qualify as a school so she went to Santa Ana and brought two of the Yoch daughters down to live at her house and attend school here. In 1904 Nick and

NAMING LAGUNA BEACH

Kathryne built a home at 289 Laguna Ave. which was shared by the family, including the author, for many years to come. Today that site is the Peacock Insurance building.

A quote from an article written in 1923 by Burton L. Smith, provides a clear window offering a view of the town through the eyes of someone who was there at the time. You can almost smell the scent of the eucalyptus trees.

"A ten-mile detour off the main highway has kept autoists away and lack of railway facilities have made invading picnickers a thing unknown. ... Whatever has been the cause Laguna has remained more near to nature than any of the Southern California beaches.

Up to two years ago the little village strung along the coast, built on crooked streets, shaded by the overhanging boughs of thickly-growing trees, gave forth the flavor of the quaint towns of the Cape Cod region. It was a bit of New England transplanted on a southern shore, quite different from any other spot in the West. A daily stage made trips from Santa Ana, the county seat, bringing the few visitors, daily supplies and mail. At the end of the winding main street was the post office. It occupied half of a large room used by a general store, and had a long high wooden porch across the front.

Here every night residents and visitors gathered in the gloaming to await the distribution of the mail. The crowd filled the store and lined the railing of the high porch outside. Many who lived up the road, Arch Beach way, or down the other direction, toward the cliffs, had wended their way over many crooked paths and carried lanterns to that they might retrace their steps without mishap. This crowd, clad in all manner of attire, indulging in a wide range of conversation, much of which was gossip, was one of the interesting things about the village. 'Waiting for the mail' every evening provided food for many recollections."[33]

Opposite Page Top: Nick Isch, Barbara Isch, Mary Isch, Mrs Isch, Kitten Isch and friends. 289 Laguna Ave.

Opposite Page Bottom: Isch home at 289 Laguna Ave. about 1919

33. Los Angeles Times. Aug 19, 1923

One of the amusing stories is about Mr. Whitten, who was town constable and was also at one time a manager of Yoch's Laguna Beach Hotel. There were two men in town who fought whenever they met, which is what happened one day out in front of the post office. Mr. Whitten, of small stature, had a rattlesnake in his hand that he had just killed. He got between the two fighters with the snake and a stick and said "*if you two ever do this again I will put you both in jail.*" The post office audience roared with delight at the morning interlude.[34]

In those days those distant neighborhoods often had one person pick up the mail for neighbors. Mrs. Bishop wrote "*I remember Mr. Wendt bringing our mail out to us to save us the long walk. He was a thoughtful, kindly neighbor.*"[35] William Wendt, a renowned painter, lived out in the southern part of Arch Beach on property which fronted what was then called "*The Old Coast Road.*" When the highway was put through there was such extensive grading that his house, stranded above the road, was forced to change its address to its present, 229 Arch Street.

The Isch store and post office building itself was of no consequence architecturally. It was just one large room with a low divider running through it to separate the store from the Post Office area. On the counter was a glass cookie jar that held "*molasses kisses,*" a candy that was chocolate on the outside and molasses inside, wrapped in red cellophane. The children of patrons were always allowed to dip into the jar. There were barrels containing sugar and flour and an old scoop.[36] Mrs. Isch used a part of the store for notions and other necessities. Old photographs reveal that the building was usually in need of fresh paint.

34. Perry McCullough "Through the Years."
35. Mrs. Joseph Bishop. South Coast News. Sept.1, 1944
36. Katherine Isch Petty, his daughter. Conversation

Uncle John Thomas near railings at Isch PO

Joe Thurston, in a series of articles he wrote in 1935 for the South Coast News, painted the following word picture.

"Nick Isch and his grocery store do not need any introduction because that was the only place where there was any activity in the village for about nine months of the year, ... The only trouble was when the mail came in and had to be sorted there wasn't anyone to wait on the customers ... if they were in any hurry the only thing to do was to leave the money on the counter for what they might want, or if they had a charge account it would be set down on a piece of paper. ... As it was an event when the mail came in most of the people would sit on the railing ... and cut nitches in it while swapping stories ... Old Uncle John Thomas, who lived in the Indiana, which he built and named after his home state, was one of the most regular figures that made use of the old railing. I think the railing suffered the greatest when he was around."[37] People in town called him Uncle because of his flowing white beard which reminded people of Uncle Sam.

"Nick started a grocery delivery route in his horse and buggy and as the people had no way of traveling except to walk this was quite an accommodation, but the horse was soon discarded and an old cut-down Ford was pressed into use." Nick never did bother to learn how to drive, so his son Maurice drove the

---

37. Joseph H. Thurston. South Coast News. Nov. 22, 1935

Maurice Isch making deliveries in horse and buggy

Car used by Maurice Isch for deliveries, in front of 289 Laguna Ave.

Ford. *"I never heard whether he ever had any trouble with the groceries staying in the machine till they arrived at their destination or not, but the roads were not very smooth and Maurice did like to drive."*[38]

Originally all of the post office boxes were inside of the building. As the town grew more boxes were needed so more were added to the outside front wall of the building. These later additions had larger doors. These were bought from Frank Miller, the builder of the Riverside Mission Inn and also Villa Rockledge here in Laguna. *"the boxes were used for the Riverside Post Office when it was located in the Rubidoux building at Seventh and Main. The equipment was owned by Frank A. Miller and was sold by him to the Laguna Post Office."*[39]

38. Joseph H. Thurston. South Coast News. Nov. 22, 1935
39. Riverside Daily Press. Aug. 19, 1921

No date was given for this sale so further research revealed the origin. "*A post office in the Rubidoux building would have to be before 1912, because the main post office was constructed then.*"[40]

All of the door-windows were opened with keys, not the dials used years later, begging the question: how many of those keys were lost in the dust over the years? In those days the postmaster had to buy and supply the equipment used in the post office. Another nostalgic touch was in the fact that those Riverside boxes still held the names of the original users, and many of those names were people who also owned homes in Laguna and were instrumental in the town's development.

When the old Isch home at 289 Laguna Avenue was torn down in the 1950s, underneath the house was found a boxful of many of the old doors for the boxes, unfortunately these were not kept. Earlier, in 1931 when the Heisler Building was built on the same corner as the old store, there was originally a patio on the Laguna Avenue side. For that patio a special lamp was made out of some of the old glass window-doors that served as the front for the boxes. It was created by Wally Joyce, a son-in-law of Nick and Kathryne Isch.

What happened to the old lamp when the patio was enclosed and became part of the building is unknown. Fortunately, the author's mother, Katherine Isch Petty (always called Kitten), also had a lamp made at that same time from four of the old post office doors, which survived and is cherished. She said that the box doors were of the larger size, so these were from the outside front porch of the building, which were the ones that had been purchased from Frank Miller of Riverside.

Photo by Johanna Ellis

40. Steve Lech, Researcher of the history of Riverside County, Ca.

While on the subject of the corner where the Isch store stood – it is true that the Heisler Building is built on the same corner – it's just that if the Isch store still existed today, it would be out in the middle of the highway, as 20 feet of the property were taken as easement to put the highway through.

Many Riverside residents helped get the town started in the right direction. Many of the homes built up the hill south of the Yoch Hotel were built on by them for their summer homes. They often brought YMCA boys to Laguna for their annual camp-out. In 1913, Elmer Jahraus, Nick Isch, and Nate Brooks provided what was needed for a Fourth of July celebration. A baseball game was played between the Riverside boys and a local Laguna team – Laguna won by 11 to 6. This group of scouts put on a play, and there being no real theater they used the front porch of the post office as their stage. There was evening dancing in the Pavilion, a small building on the Yoch Hotel property.[41]

Laguna finds patronage largely in the conservative class, who never tire of the quiet but unchangeable beauties of the coast and sea.

It is the opinion of its devotees that it will be a sad day for Laguna when it gets a railroad, for then the vulgar crowd and all its other accessories will deal it a death blow.

Nature has generously endowed this little place, therefore a lavishness of human nature would be superfluous.

Some time this place will be a mecca for artists.

— Riverside Daily Press, 1899

41. Riverside Daily Press. July 7, 1913

Florence Yoch, Mary Isch, Marie at side of Isch Post Office

FLORENCE YOCH

The Youngest of six Yoch daughters, Florence went on to become a world-famous landscape architect, doing private homes of Pasadena and Montecito estates. She did the gardens for the homes of Jack Warner, George Cukor and David Selznick, and the movie sets for Tara, in "Gone With The Wind" and the movie "Romeo and Juliet."

Credit: LB Historical Society

THE CISTERN

When Marriner was building his Stationary Store at 225 Forest Ave. the builders ran into something near the back door, which faced Park Avenue, that they couldn't explain. They went up to see Nick Isch to see if he could add any light. He explained that at one time there had been a cistern at that exact spot. Every time you see that door that is still there you will be able to picture old Laguna full of trees.

GETTING THE MAIL INTO TOWN

"NEITHER SNOW NOR RAIN NOR HEAT..."

Of all the people associated in one way or another with the post office, the men bringing the mail into town deserve great credit. In those early years meeting the train at El Toro and then making the trip in a buggy or a horse-drawn stagecoach down a dirt path through Laguna Canyon or Aliso Canyon took dedicated effort. The rainy season would have brought rushing water in the creek, flooding, muddy ruts, and chilling to the bone. The summer produced mustard plants that were shoulder high, with dust and weeds everywhere. Travelers often complained of a couple of places where the sandy spots made it difficult for buggy wheels to traverse. Drivers always carried a rifle or shotgun to defend from attack from wildcats and robbers. While research has yet to reveal a complete list of names of those who signed contracts for mail delivery to Laguna, there are numerous written articles and stories told of the experiences of this hardy lot who provided such a basic need for the town.

The first name mentioned was Lorraine Thrall making mail delivery to the Arch Beach Post Office during its short existence. This post office was part of the hotel, named "Arch

Arch Beach Hotel

Beach House," located on the cliff overlooking Woods Cove. His son, Will Thrall, fourteen years old at the time, wrote of their experiences.

The family moved to Arch Beach in July of 1888, where they had the boarding stable for horses and the stage route to El Toro. They lived in a small house with a dirt floor. His father let young Will follow his adventurous spirit, allowing him to drive the two-horse stage twelve miles through Aliso Canyon to El Toro and even ocassionally allowed him to drive the four-horse vehicle twenty-two passengers rig.

Driving the mail route one day he encountered a twenty-eight pound bobcat. Grabbing his rifle he quickly fired upon the cat but only wounded it and it rushed the boy, who fought it off with his bare fists and was finally able to subdue the animal with the butt of his rifle.

On another occasion he and his father, Lorraine, were travelling through Aliso Canyon where they stopped to observe a rattlesnake "charming" a bobcat. Lorraine shot the snake, but not before the snake got his fangs into the cat. On

Lorraine and son Will Thrall (top) and family

another occasion young Will, while delivering the mail, was later trapped by flooding waters caused by a large rainstorm which he escaped by scrambling to the top of a nearby hill. He later wrote a first-hand account of the heavy storms that hit California in December 1889-1890, when it had rained for twenty continuous days. He gave a vivid account of the continual storms that destroyed almost all of the roads, bridges, and railroad lines in the area.[42]

42. "Will Thrall and the San Gabriels – A Man to Match the Mountains" by Ronald C. Woolsey. Copyright 2004, San Diego Sunbelt Publications. A large thank you to Mark Whitman who provided the information to me about the Thralls.

Fernando Farman, who moved to Laguna in 1892, was the first stage coach driver in Laguna Beach. He stored the coach in the old Ponder's Barn on Laguna Ave. There is a story that after the arrival of motor-driven vehicles and the demise of horse-drawn stage coaches his "Concord" stage was used by a film crew that drove it over the cliff at Aliso Creek. He also had a smaller buggy that he used for transporting people to their destinations. There is a picture of him with Madam Modjeska taken at the depot in El Toro.

Soon after the Brooks Hotel burned down in 1893, William Brooks was awarded the contract to deliver U.S. mail from El Toro to Arch Beach.[43] For delivery of the mail and passengers to Laguna in 1895, the stagecoach met the 9:55 a.m. southbound train at El Toro on Tuesday, Thursday and Saturday from November 1 to June 1. For the summer schedule, from June 1 to the last of October, the stage ran daily except on Sundays. Will Brooks had this contract and he announced that he had reduced the fare to 25 cents, and baggage was free.[44]

> In going to Luguna Beach, take U. S. mail stage at El Toro. Safe and reliable. Fare 25c. W. H. Brooks, owner and driver.   ju20m2

William Brooks ad for stage coach

In 1897, some of the four-year contracts for carrying mail were about to expire, Lagona's included. Bidding was opened for July 1, 1898, to July 1, 1902. From El Toro to Lagona, nine miles and back, six times a week. It required a

43. Los Angeles Times. April 27, 1894
44. Los Angeles Times. July 17, 1895

Madam Modjeska and Fernando Farman at El Toro Depot

bond of $700, and the present contract price was $250.20.[45] Though Will Brooks did drive the stage to Laguna for years, he sold his property and moved away from Laguna in 1900. He did return to town around 1913.[46]

The horse-drawn stagecoach era came to an end in 1909. Widespread use of the reliable automobile marked an irreversible change in America's transportation, and Laguna and it's isolated off-the-beaten path existence was doomed to change in the years ahead. The Yochs tested using automotive passenger carriers from Santa Ana to their Laguna Beach Hotel. It proved successful.

The postal inspector had approved the use of the machine for mail delivery, and had approved two deliveries a day to Laguna. The mail delivery from El Toro would continue for a short time, and the second mail delivery would

45. Los Angeles Times. September 18, 1897
46. Letter from his son, Clarence. Aug. 17, 1966

Fred, Ernie and Ada Trefren Hauling Water Main Beach about 1900
Credit: LB Historical Society

come from Santa Ana, rather than El Toro. The thirty-five horsepower machine made the twenty-mile trip from Santa Ana in just under two hours.[47]

July 1, 1910, marked the last delivery of mail from El Toro to Laguna.

"On July 1 the old Laguna-El Toro stage will be a thing of the past."[48] A new depot had been built at Irvine and from that date on the new mail carrier, Fred Trefren, would deliver the mails by his auto transfer. They did go on to say that the ride from Santa Ana to Laguna these days was full of charm. There had been a large planting of walnut trees on the Irvine Ranch and the ride would be through productive orchards.

Fred Trefren is another name that deserves to appear more in the histories of Laguna's early days. Joe Thurston said that Trefren had acquired a number of lots in the area south of Park Ave., about halfway between town and the schoolhouse. He traded his lots with Joe Yoch for two passenger cars and a truck, and started to haul passengers and freight from Santa Ana. "He was a familiar sight along these roads, where he gained quite a reputation as an Irish wit."[49]

His son, Ernie Trefren, was involved in Laguna's village life also. In 1914, he built a dance hall that was then located on First. St. - today's address would be 302 Glenneyre.

47. Los Angeles Times. Sept. 6, 1909
48. Riverside Daily Press. June 20, 1910
49. "Laguna Beach of Early Days." Joseph Thurston

Young Thelma Farman had staged a dance performance there which was one of Lynn Aufdenkamp's earliest memories of her. By 1917, Trefren and Whistler opened a meat and fish market on Forest Ave.

In 1964 Mrs. John Robbins Lucas and her brother John Brenot provided information for an article in the South Coast News. They spent their early childhood in Laguna and remembered many of the facts from that time. According to the article they claimed the old stage line was officially known as the "Laguna Auto Transfer" and was operated by Mrs. Lucas' step-father, Oscar Warling, in partnership with Fred Trefren.

Oscar Warling stage on Old Coast Road on way to Capistrano

Oscar Warling, left, at Mission

One of the autos was a "Tourist" and another was a "Rapid Truck" and was used to haul freight. The third was a "Thomas Flier." These operated out of a livery stable run by Oscar Warling and Nick Isch. This livery stable later became the town's first garage and gas station. Brenot told of how he used to go to Santa Ana to bring back drums of gasoline, which he bought for four cents a gallon

First gas station. Today 329 South Coast Highway

and sold for six cents a gallon. Originally the gas was poured into auto tanks from a five-gallon can. Later the garage installed one pump.[50]

A 1916 notice in the local newspaper "Laguna Life" stated that due to rain *"Laguna was without mail service either in or out through Irvine from Tuesday until Thursday night. Roy Peacock brought in the first load. Hail Peacock."*[51] In 1919, once again William Brooks is mentioned because he was on vacation and in his absence the mail was being brought to town by Fred Clapp.[52] In 1924 the Chamber of Commerce publicly thanked Ed Hofer for his many years of carrying the mail. Joe Skidmore said *"I always set my watch by his coming and going."*[53]

In early newspapers there are several ads for different stage drivers. These were of course automobile stages by then. Not all the stage lines were involved with delivering mail - their main purpose was to bring supplies and people, to Laguna.

50. South Coast News. Feb. 28, 1964.
51. Laguna Life. January 21, 1916
52. South Coast News. Sept. 22, 1936. "Laguna Years Ago."
53. Laguna Life. Oct. 24, 1924.

1917

KING & FRASIER
Laguna Beach
STAGE LINE
Schedule
[Effective June 18, 1917]

Leave Laguna	Leave Santa Ana
6:00 a.m.	8:15 a.m.
7:30 a.m.	9:15 a.m.
10:30 a.m.	2:15 p.m.
2:15 p.m.	4:15 p.m.
4:00 p.m.	5:15 p.m.

Special Sunday Night Car will Leave Laguna Beach at 6:30 p.m.

Laguna Beach Offices
KING AND FRASIER GARAGE
Laguna Beach Pharmacy.

Santa Ana Offices
White Cross Drug Store
Both Phones 42

Salt Lake Railway Office.
Both Phones 211

Light Freight and Express Service in Connection

1915

TIME TABLE
PEACOCK'S LAGUNA AND ARCH BEACH STAGE.

Three trips daily

Leaves Laguna Beach at 7:30 and 10:30 A. M. and 4:00 P.M. Leaves Santa Ana at 9:15 A. M. and 2:15 and 5:15 P. M. Leave orders at Peacock's Garage, Laguna Beach, Calif.

—o—

DRURY & KING
Laguna and Arch Beach Stage

Leaves Laguna.	Leaves Santa Ana.
7:30 a. m.	10.15 a. m.
4.00 p. m.	5:15 p. m.

Light freight, express and baggage to and from Santa Ana and Irvine.

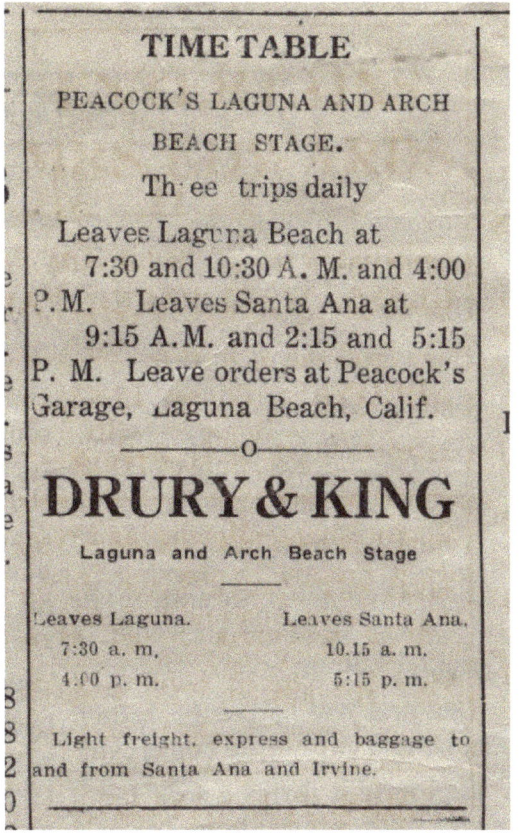

Peacock's Laguna and Arch Beach Stage to California's most beautiful Scenic Beach.

New, modern 7-passenger stages leave Santa Ana for Laguna Beach at 9:15, 10 15 A M. and 2:15, 4.15, 5:15 P.M. Connecting with Pacific Electric, Santa Fe and Southern Pacific trains. Round trip fare, $1.00.

If convenient, please reserve your seats by mail or phone. Santa Ana Office, White Cross Drug Store, Cor. 4th and Sycamore sts. Both Phones 42. Laguna Beach Office, Peacock's Laguna Beach Garage. P. O. Box address Box 59. BE SURE IT'S PEACOCK'S STAGE

1916

CHANGING POSTMASTERS

After so many years of tending to stamps, money orders, and packages, it was time for Nick Isch to retire as postmaster. His retirement was announced in June of 1920. Though no longer postmaster, the post office continued to be in his store for another three years.

Blanche B. Brown took over as Postmaster on October 1, 1920.[54] Blanche Boulanger Brown was a widow who had grown up in Missouri. When Laguna's Art Association was formed in 1918 she was the first custodian-curator in the small gallery on the Hotel property.[55]

By 1919, she had an innovative idea that would be popular today. Her plan was to build what she named *"Toy Village"* consisting of ten small studios in a courtyard setting that would be available to artists only. She had purchased property at the extreme north-west corner of Laguna Cliffs, looking into Divers' Cove, Fishermen's Cove and Boat Canyon. These studio-apartment quarters were to be in the old French chateau style. No two would be alike and they would be painted different light colors. *"No two will be erected on the same level, the topography of the sight (sic) permits of winding pathways, many steps and a variety that will give the place a uniqueness little seen outside of French chateaus."*[56] Well, two did get built, and she sold those in May of 1920.[57]

Unfortunately she died on December 20, 1920, only two months after becoming Postmaster. Therefore Nick went back to handling the mails temporarily.

54. Santa Ana Register. Oct. 2, 1920
55. Santa Ana Register. July 1, 1919
56. Santa Ana Register. June 9, 1919.
57. Santa Ana Register. May 13, 1920

In January of 1921, there was a public notice in the local newspaper that The Civil Service Commission was going to hold examinations that month for a postmaster at Laguna Beach. The post office was of the *"fourth class,"* and the pay at that office for the last fiscal year was $678. A follow-up article stated that *"the postmaster is expected to furnish the letterboxes, as well as other necessary paraphernalia. The boxes in the recently furnished post office cost $200."*[58] The paper said this not to discourage applicants but just to let it be known that it would take at least $300 to get up and running.

The local paper had another announcement for another examination scheduled for July 1921, for postmaster at Laguna. Laguna had grown and now rated as a Third Class Post office and would pay the postmaster $1,200.[59] On July 1, 1921, Brayton S. Norton was appointed acting postmaster. His Presidential appointment came through in October of 1921.

Brayton Norton was well-known to local residents. His family was among the early settlers from Riverside who built homes on the hill above the Hotel and he had been coming to Laguna since he was a young boy. He loved to write and penned a play - actually a spoof - titled "Machamlock" that he subtitled "A Shakespearian Mix-Up In Three Spasms." Its 1908 performance by local talent was certainly one of the earliest recorded plays to be staged in Laguna.

The program reveals that the actors for the roles were played by many well-known Laguna names – Moulton, Ferris, Jahraus, Skidmore and others. The scenery was painted by Conway Griffith, the first artist to make Laguna his permanent home. The novel *"El Diablo"* was written by Brayton Norton as well as short stories for Argosy Magazine.[60] One

58. Laguna Life. Jan. 7, 1921
59. Laguna Life. July 1, 1921
60. Alibris, website

"MACHAMLOCK"
A Shakespearian Mix-Up in Three Spasms
By Brayton S. Norton
Time--8:15 P. M.

CAST OF CHARACTERS (In Order of Appearance)

Macbeth, Thane of Irvine	Joe Skidmore
Lady Macbeth	Pauline Jahraus
Shylock, a Jew of Balboa	Brayton Norton
Hamlet, the Mad Prince of El Toro	Joe Jahraus
Ophelia, Also Mad	Florence Yoch
Ghost of Hamlet's Father	John P. Norton
Citizen	Arthur Moulton
First Witch	Dorothy Cunningham
Second Witch	Bertha Van Zwalenburg
Third Witch	Helen G. Norton
Portia, a Corporation Lawyer	Ethel L. Smith
Nerissa, Portia's Stenographer	Helen G. Norton
Ernie Gobbo, the Office Boy	Ferris Moulton

SYNOPSIS OF SCENERY

ACT I. Scene 1—A Street in Laguna. Scene 2—Shylock's Butcher Shop, Not in a Trust. Scene 3—A Laguna Restaurant. Scene 4—Willis Street, Laguna Beach. Scene 5—Shylock's Shop.

ACT II. Scene 1—Shylock's Butcher Shop. Scene 2—Trefren Street, Laguna Beach. Scene 3—The Devil's Blow Hole. Scene 4—Portia's Law Office.

ACT III. Scene 1—A Court of Justice. Scene 2—Jahraus Street, Laguna Beach. Scene 3—A Room in Portia's House.

Executive Staff

Stage Manager	John P. Norton
Stage Carpenter	J. Derkum

Appreciation

¶ The Cast wish to express their sincerest appreciation of Nastia Lark's kindness, for the use of a number of the costumes used in this play; also of the work of Conway Griffith in painting the scenery.

Credit: Thelma and Lynn Aufdenkamp

of his novels was made into a movie titled "*Sleeping Acres*" starring Wallace Beery and Rex "Snowy" Baker."[61] He would be postmaster for the next 13 years. Later he would serve the town for many years with the Laguna Beach County Water District and he was active in the Presbyterian Church.

The post office was still in the Isch store and Norton began making more room for the mailing needs of the growing population of Laguna. First, in October of 1921, he extended to the ceiling what had been a low wall separating the store from the mail area.[62] In 1922, he doubled the amount of room used for the post office.[63] Apparently there was very little room left for groceries.

Ninteen twenty-three marked the beginning of a period of rapid growth to come. Everyone knew that the opening of a highway to Newport was only a matter of time and that would bring the end of this idyllic period. Property values were on the rise, but the town still had no bank. Small quaint Laguna was starting to change.

Where the Glenneyre Parking structure is today was to be the site of "*The Villas*," a bunch of small cabins, in a eucalyptus grove, with winding paths. The administration building for these was to be built on the corner of the old Isch store. Directly across the street from that, on the north east corner of Laguna Avenue and the highway of today, the Yoch Company was erecting a building (it is still there.)

The Murphy Building had been finished the previous year, at the north-east corner of the highway and Ocean Ave.—also still there—and both spots were trying to win approval from Washington to house the Post Office. The Yoch Building was chosen. The front of the building was to house

---

61. San Francisco Chronicle. Aug. 14, 1921 and IMDB
62. Laguna Life. Oct. 28, 1921
63. Laguna Life. March 10, 1922

The Villas office bldg. 1924 later a restaurant. SE corner of laguna ave. and highway. Isch home roof line at left. credit First American Title Co.

the new bank – Laguna's first. The small section behind that was for the local paper, Laguna Life, and some office space, and the rest, rear part of the building, was the new post office.

"Postmaster Norton stated that when the post office is moved into the new Yoch building there will be an entire new outfit of fixtures including boxes enough to meet all requirements: also that the latter will be of the latest improved keyless kind. Just another indication of how 'the beach that is different' is becoming different."[64]

Just before this happened the old building was to appear one last time. *"The lamented post office of Laguna Beach is in the last ditch but is making an heroic plea for fame this week as it makes an important scene in the Ince camera while Peter B. Kyne's story, 'Bar Harbor' is being shot."*[65]

Directed by W.H. Van Dyke, the film starred Monte Blue and Evelyn Brent with Charles Gerrard cast as the villain. The whole contingent from Hollywood consisted of about

64. Laguna Life. June 8, 1923
65. Laguna Life. June 1, 1923

NAMING LAGUNA BEACH

Yoch bldg. built 1923 with new PO at rear, on Laguna Ave. 2 men leaning on front wall of new bank. Now 390 South Coast Highway. Credit: First American Title Insurance Co.

100 people who were all staying at the Laguna Beach Hotel. The following account of life in this small village appeared in the Santa Ana Register.

"Monday evening the whole of Laguna and Arch Beach turned out en masse to watch the shooting of storm scenes on the village street. Brilliant lights and reflectors were set up on the boulevard beside the art gallery and powerful streams of water shot into the air which came down as very wet and realistic rain, blown about by gusts from a wind machine. The great waste of water caused much agitation among property owners until they were reassured by an accommodating member of the company that it's out of the sea. You can taste it if you want to."[66]

This article points out probably the biggest single problem facing residents and visitors alike—lack of decent water. What was being piped down from the canyon was of terrible quality, and worst of all the wells were beginning to run alarmingly dry.

66. Santa Ana Register. May 30, 1923

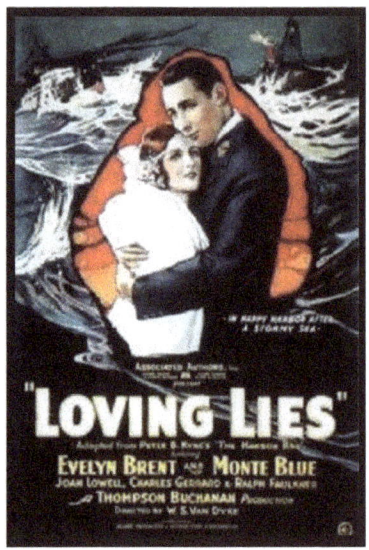

And talk about problems, Monte Blue ended up in the hospital for several days which held up production of the film. The script called for Monte, who refused a double for the scene, to make a landing on the rugged beach during a heavy squall. A large wave hit the boat and threw him into the ocean, and a second wave threw the boat against him, breaking a rib and causing many bruises.[67] When the movie was released the title had changed to "Loving Lies."[68]

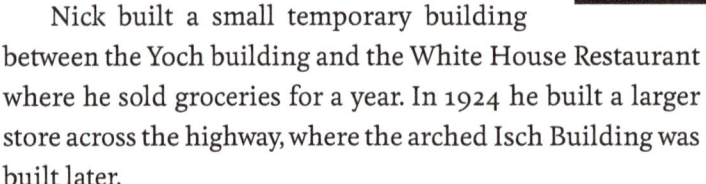

Loving Lies movie poster

Nick built a small temporary building between the Yoch building and the White House Restaurant where he sold groceries for a year. In 1924 he built a larger store across the highway, where the arched Isch Building was built later.

All indications are that the old original store was probably torn down, though never was it described that way—,only that it was a thing of the past. Local boy Bud Watkins said that he remembered that it had been moved off its original foundation and placed temporarily next door. Years later, an article written by Lorraine Pardee Fisher stated that *"The original post office and general store rose to the rank of cottage. It was bought by two energetic sisters, carried to their particular lot, plunked warpily down and bedecked with partitions, very sketchy plumbing and a balcony - all constructed by the ladies. It waves gracefully when the wind blows and leaks copiously when it rains, but it is 'artistic' and, better still, historic."*[69] To this day historians wonder if it still exists, long since remodeled, added to or changed.

67. Plain Dealer (Cleveland, Oh) August 12, 1923
68. A copy of the old film has not been found.
69. South Coast News. Festival Edition. 1946. P.8

Isch Store June 1923 till July 3, 1924, moved across the highway. Building at right was offce bldg. for the Villas, later a restauraunt, later site of Heisler Bldg. 2 men still leaning on front of bank building. Credit: First America Title Insurance Co.

In 1940, there was a brief reappearance of the old Isch store on the grounds of the Festival of Arts. The Ebell Club, under the direction of Mrs. Gates W. Burrows, was sponsoring and creating a booth reproducing the old store, and Nick Isch would be there on the porch to welcome old-timers and give new-comers a glance back into Laguna's early days.[70]

Festival of arts grounds, 1940 reenactment of Isch Store and PO

70. Santa Ana Register. July 16, 1940

BIGGEST RUSH

Kitten and Jane Petty. Hotel Laguna garden. Ebell Fashion Show 1945 old post office reenactment. South Coast News May 17, 1945

"The old post office is now a thing of the past, and we are receiving our mail in the new office, where Postmaster Norton is gradually bringing order out of chaos Within a few days everything will be working smoothly, and we will become accustomed to the keyless boxes, the separate slots for local, out-of-state and eastern mail and the nice clean bulletin board on which Brayton will post notices of things which, in the judgment of "the powers that be" in Washington, we should know. No provision has been made for posting lost or found articles, so we suppose that the things that are lost will have to stay lost."[71]

In 1923, there were two regular employees at the post office. For the Christmas rush two under-aged young ladies were brought in to help get the mails done on time.

---

71. Laguna Life. June 23, 1923

Above: Catherine Cravath in front of Isch home, Ponders barn across street

Top Right: Barbara Isch and Catherine Cravath Ponders Barn Across Laguna Ave.

Katherine Isch, seventeen-year-old daughter of the previous postmaster, and Catherine Cravath, daughter of Gavy Cravath, helped get the packages and mail sorted.[72] The two had been friends for years.

Even more surprising is that the next summer Postmaster Norton and his wife were leaving for a vacation to Bishop where he expected to spend much of his time-off fishing and hunting. Wondering who will be acting postmaster while Norton was gone? Nick Isch's daughter Katherine Isch, always called Kitten, home from UCLA for her vacation.[73]

Returning from his trip, Norton's next order of business was to start twice-daily mail pick-ups and deliveries, which included the need to keep the doors open for longer periods of time.

Catherine Cravath, center, and Kitten Isch next. Park Ave. Two-room shcoolhouse fence

72. Laguna Life. Dec. 28, 1923
73. Laguna Life. Aug. 18, 1924

It's difficult to picture what it was like to have to go to the post office to get or send your mail–there was still no home delivery in 1924. At this time the Post Office Department signed a new delivery contract with Crown Stage Company for $1,080 per year which would bring the mail directly from Santa Ana. The old Star Mail Route between Laguna and Irvine was abandoned meaning that Ed Hofer would no longer be bringing in the mail. Brayton Norton paid special tribute to him, "*I am sincerely sorry that Ed Hofer is the loser by this new contract. He has given good service. His willingness to wait for mails beyond the time set in the contract, that the people of Laguna Beach might not be disappointed, deserves special mention. Ed Hofer gave 100 percent service, no matter what the weather.*"[74]

By 1925, continued growth made it necessary to add more space to the post office. The front of the building facing the highway was still the Citizen's Bank. The post office was at the rear, the entrance door being on Laguna Avenue. In between, previously, there had been office space and store rooms. That space was being taken over by the post office, making it necessary for Joe Thurston to find a different space for his desk.

The Yoch Company, owner of the building, agreed to do the necessary alterations. The present partition containing the drops, money-order and general delivery windows were to be turned so that the drops were next to the door.

Kitten Isch. Tennis courts were next door to Edgar Payne studio on the left on Glenneyre. Courts today would be 510 Glenneyre

74. Laguna Life. Oct.17, 1924

82 NAMING LAGUNA BEACH

Norton ordered one hundred more boxes, bringing the total to five hundred and twenty-five. There was room for addition of one hundred more boxes when that became necessary. In the old Isch post office and store there had been only thirty-six boxes.[75] A mild uproar occurred when the cost of renting boxes was increased from .35, .45, and .60 cents to .45, .60, and .75 cents. Norton had to restore order by assuring patrons he did not keep any of that money and that all of it went directly to Washington, and that the rate was set according to how much business was done. What Lagunans paid forty-five cents for cost residents in Santa Ana one dollar. Another blow was dealt to a convenience for residents – from then on the clerks would hand over a neighbor's mail only on written consent from the owner of the box.[76]

"Post Office Has Biggest Rush in History" headlined the local newspaper in 1925. All eighty sacks of mail were received. Postmaster Norton, his wife Edna, Harriet Boulanger and Pauline Jahraus *"worked all day like beavers and by closing time but few of the bundles remained."*

Norton praised Lagunans for mailing early.[77] If the name Harriet Boulanger rings a bell it is because she was a sister of Blanche Boulanger Brown, previous postmaster who served for such a short time.

Recall that at this time Laguna's roads were not paved and they still followed the natural contours of the land. Laguna Avenue still sloped downhill and cars were sliding sideways and hitting cars parked in front of the post office. On a muddy rainy day this was a particularly big problem, so Traffic Officer Howell installed a no parking sign in front of the post office.[78]

75. Laguna Life. May 1, 1925
76. Laguna Life. July 3, 1925
77. News Post. Turn Back the Clock. Dec. 24, 1975
78. Laguna Beach Life. Aug.7, 1925

Laguna was forever changed after 1926 - the highway to Newport, even though only an unpaved dirt road spread with oil, was opened which meant a large increase in the traffic and population of Laguna. No longer was the only road into town Laguna Canyon Road.

Postal receipts jumped 51% from the previous year of 1925. Norton frequently used postal receipts to give estimations of the population in town, in this case an increase from 1,500 last year to 2,200 this year.[79]

A note about population figures. Over the years it is difficult to be certain, and or even compare with certainty the numbers quoted. Much depends on the area being used in the count. The Canyon, Temple Hills, anything south of Victoria Beach, and surrounding neighborhoods in Laguna were still in the county, and were not used in figuring the population of Laguna. So to compare them to today's numbers can be misleading.

Another turning point in Laguna's history occurred in 1927, for that is when the town incorporated. Growth brought about another change in that year - the post office jumped from third class to second class status. This jump meant that better service would be rendered. From now on the employees would be recruited through the civil service. The windows would be open all day - previously they had to close while the sorting of the mail took place.[80]

The Postal Inspectors still refused to allow free delivery to residences due to Laguna's special topography and the fact that the dirt roads lacked sidewalks. This, coupled with the fact that the present building lacked enough room, brought about the idea to build a new large post office as there was no building in town large enough to accommodate the needs.

79. Santa Ana Register. Dec.10, 1926
80. Los Angeles Times. Jan.8, 1927

Laguna Ave. dirt slide zone after 1923.
Credit: First American Title Insurance Co.

Many prominent businessmen in town came forward with offers to build a new building.[81] That didn't happen. Instead the Yoch Company signed a long-term contract that would involve enlarging the existing space to the required one thousand, five hundred square feet.[82]

One of the ways to alleviate the long distances that patrons were travelling to get and send their mail was to open a branch office in Arch Beach. By 1929, Postmaster Norton listed in the local paper all the qualifications that must be met for that to happen.[83]

It didn't happen, not yet.

And still the car-crashing problem continued on unpaved Laguna Avenue. Six cars in six months was a figure just too high, so the city fathers decreed anyone parking on Laguna Avenue between the highway and Ramona would be going before the judge.[84]

81. Santa Ana Register. March 18, 1927
82. Los Angeles Times. July 15, 1927
83. Laguna Beach Life. Jan. 25, 1929
84. South Coast News. May 17, 1929

Parking lot on corner of Laguina Ave and Park Ave. Now site of Library. Side of PO building on left side of photo.

The Great Depression had deepened by 1933, and the local post office clerks had been forced to have three payless furlough days a month.[85] Even so, the mail receipts continued to grow and more space was needed.

In January, Smith Brothers Construction had just completed another remodeling of the Yoch Building, now owned by Edgar B. McKnight. He had a ten-year lease agreement with the government. The wall between the post office and the next store had been torn down and this had doubled amount of space allowing the addition of three hundred new boxes, bringing the total to one thousand, five hundred and a U-shaped lobby was created.[86] Norton reported that many post offices across the country had dropped back in receipts but Laguna showed an increase of 12% over the previous year. *"The raise in first class rates from two to three cents had not brought the increase in revenue that was expected."*[87]

For years there was a triangular-shaped empty lot right next to the post office. It was empty because the old Ponder's barn had since been torn down. It provided a convenience

85. South Coast News. Sept. 1, 1933
86. South Coast News. June 16, 1933
87. Santa Ana Register. July 14, 1933

to patrons, as there was no parking in front of the post office. Over Labor Day of 1933, the Los Angeles owner of the lot came down to Laguna, and was unable to park in his own lot. Right after that a fence went up around it.[88] Much later, that lower part of Park Avenue was closed off to provide enough space for a new Library. Part of the library of today is built on that odd-sized parking lot.

Time for a change, and in 1933 it was Ada E. Purpus who was endorsed by the Democratic county central committee meeting in Santa Ana, after considering all the possibilities[89]. Ada Purpus became postmaster on Oct.22, 1934.[90]

Mrs. Purpus could boast about one of her staff members. John W. Marriner had recently returned from Los Angeles where he participated in a "*case examination.*" The test was to memorize the locations of 836 towns in California in such a way that they could throw mail destined to these places into 35 different pigeon holes within a limited amount of time. Mr. Marriner scored a bullseye every time.[91]

88. South Coast News. Oct. 27, 1933
89. South Coast News. Nov.24, 1933
90. Official Post Office Records. National Archives
91. South Coast News. March 3, 1934

There was another attempt to have a sub-station in Arch Beach, again to no avail[92]. The big issue at this time was the attempt to get mail delivery. Even after ten years of trying, the latest application had been made and turned down by Washington. The City Council asked to have Mrs. Purpus pass on their objection to Washington.[93]

What appears to have perhaps turned the tide was a letter written by Henry J. Weeks, who lived in Arch Beach, with an accompanying petition sent to the Assistant Postmaster General in Washington. Weeks pointed out many details about their claim of "deficiency of funds" due to the Depression and asked many questions. He gave a vivid description of *"retired old people of scanty means having to trudge from one to two miles along the crowded state boulevard (the only way to the post office) filled with motorists....and then, after reaching the post office, to compel these tired and weary people to wait at the one solitary open service window, for from 15 to 30 minutes before they are served."*[94]

He expected the New Deal to be applied to Laguna's residents in the form of a long overdue free delivery service, and was sending a copy of his letter to the President, Postmaster General, Senator McAdoo and Congressman Collins with a request for immediate action. Surely that heart-breaking description would bring favorable results.

In the local paper a little over a week later there appeared the following telegram from Congressman Collins *"The Laguna Beach application for city delivery service has been reopened by the post office department and an investigation is*

---

92.   South Cost News. Jan 18, 1935

93.   South Coast News. April 19, 1935

94.   South Coast News. May 3, 1935

in progress. Have telegraphed inspector at San Diego and he has promised to expedite his report. Hope to secure a reversal of the former unfavorable action by the department."[95]

The reply was not long in coming. *"Mrs. Ada E. Purpus, postmaster, was pleased to announce that she has received information from Washington that city delivery will be installed in Laguna Beach October 1, 1935, this contingent upon patrons providing house numbers and mail boxes."*[96] That was a big if.

There had been no house numbering prior to this time period, a fact which has made historical research difficult at times. For years people named their houses - a list of those would provide many a chuckle. A few examples were *The Lifted Latch, Wickiup, Snugglein, Dunwander Cottage, Iowana, Stepping Stones, El Shacko* and my favorite, *Sag Rafters*.

Air castle sign - Sleepy Hollow- Don Lay-1925

In 1916 under "Want Ads" there was a listing that said *"I paint signs for your summer cottages. Also small oil sketches of local Laguna scenery, and weave artistic Eucalyptus baskets. Helen Irene Welles, Inwood Cottage."*[97]

In 1928, on the recommendation of a committee made up of City Engineer A.J. Stead and Frank S. Browne, the newly established City Council had passed an ordinance requiring the citizens to designate their houses by number rather than name. *"Laguna Beach, like many resort towns or summer cities, has not been conducted along the staid and set lines of more sedate communities. Residents have exercised their imaginations in naming*

95. South Coast News. May 17, 1935
96. South Coast News. Sept. 6, 1935
97. Laguna Life. Aug. 4, 1916

*their homes, and many fanciful appelations have been used."*⁹⁸ Ada Purpus had reason to worry.

Henry J. Weeks was acknowledged as having played a prominent part in getting mail delivery, and it was believed that he was the first person who placed his order for a mail box with the Laguna Lumber Co.

Now the push was on to get the citizens to buy and install mailboxes and number their houses. To meet the first of October date for free delivery, at least seventy-five percent of the boxes and house numbers had to be in place by September twentieth. On that date the routes would be established, and lack of number and box would imply the resident didn't want free delivery. Postmaster Purpus was hopeful that citizens would act immediately and that notification of installation would be filed at the post office.⁹⁹

There was deep worry that if Lagunans didn't get their house numbers and boxes in order that it would be years before the town would ever again be considered for free delivery. Henry Weeks asked the local paper to publish a letter he had received from Senator Hiram W. Johnson, dated August 31, 1935.

In part, the letter said that regulation mail boxes of galvanized iron for the district north of Laguna Cliffs and south of Sleepy Hollow cost only $1.00 plus a few cents for placing them on the curb, at a height to be reached by the mail carrier from his car without dismounting. For the business district mail boxes cost between twenty cents to sixty cents.

98. Santa Ana Register. Aug. 27, 1928
99. South Coast News. Sept 7, 1935

There was of course another worry. This was Laguna after all, and having a contingent of artists living here the subject arose concerning all those ugly boxes stuck on top of posts that would create eyesores. Virginia Wooley, local artist, wrote a charming article for the local paper titled "*Beauty for Mail Boxes.*"

"*Now, a post with a box on top of it need not be homely, nor even conspicuous. Many plans are being made by the artists to camouflage these necessary additions, and I'll pass on a few of their ideas.*"

A shrub planted in such a way that the box will have a background, with soft green paint the tone of the bush, or a little trellis house with a new vine would quickly cover the trellis, or even plant a tree and attach the box, which has been painted the color of the tree trunk, were some of the suggestions. "*Don't hesitate to sign up, just see how well you can disguise it and make it a thing of beauty.*"[100]

There must have been a run on mailboxes and house numbers at the Jahraus Lumber Yard, because with a sigh of relief mail delivery did begin on time. Delivery started that Tuesday with three carriers. The post office was amazed - the lines at the post office were as long as ever on Tuesday and Wednesday.[101]

By January 1936, collection mail boxes were being installed at strategic spots around town. Concrete posts were embedded in the sidewalks near the curbs.

As early as 1938, the town was requesting a new post office building. It didn't happen that year as the town had hoped it would. In 1939, new regulations were passed that required that all postmasters be selected by civil service examination, and Mrs. Purpus had become postmaster by appointment.

100. South Coast News. Sept. 27, 1935
101. South Coast News. Oct. 4, 1935

There were eleven, yes eleven, people seeking the position.

The test was to be given at the high school. Taking the test were local residents William S. Caldwell, Leo B. Wilson, Mrs. Agnes A. Peck, Henry W. Hall, Mrs. Ann T. Rhoades, Francis E. Miller, Emanuel Moog, Emerson B. Milnor, Michael F. Noone, Caroline Yoch Barnett, and Mrs. Ada Purpus. Surprisingly, Mrs. Purpus was the only one to pass the test. By August the position was still up in the air because the policy was to take the top three people who passed and decide from that group who would be given the position, and Washington didn't know what to do under the circumstances of there being only one possibility.[102] By January of 1940, it was all settled and Ada Purpus would continue as postmaster. Acting upon recommendation of President Roosevelt, the Senate approved her appointment.[103]

In 1939, once again the subject came up for having a post office station out to the south in Arch Beach. Mrs. Purpus opened the bidding on June 1, and she listed the requirements. The station would have to *"provide all necessary equipment including screened office, sign, safe, heat, light and all clerical services necessary for the conduct of such a station."*[104] Contract Station No. 1 was opened July 1, 1939, at 1956 Coast Blvd. South. The contract had been awarded to Mrs. Don Wilkie. *"It will carry stamps and postal supplies, money orders will be issued and paid, and parcel post and registered mail will be accepted daily except Sunday, between the hours of 8 a.m. and 6 p.m.*[105] Henry Weeks, who lived on Bluebird Canyon Drive, probably had a big smile on his face.

102. South Coast News. Aug. 29, 1939
103. South Coast News. Jan. 19, 1940
104. South Coast News. May 3, 1939
105. South Coast News. June 27, 1939

Contract Station No. 1
1968 S. Coast. Highway.
Credit: Los Angeles
Public Library

SET IN STONE

In early 1941, because of the large Christmas rush and the fact that there had been large annual increases in volume, it was approved by Washington to build a new larger post office in Laguna. All bids had to be in by January 15.

"As postal inspectors for this district are well acquainted with possible sites in Laguna, no delay is expected to be encountered in awarding the contract to the successful bidder."[106]

Several possible sites had been put forward, and one of the most important requirements was for ample parking space and easy egress and ingress for mail delivery conveyances. The final choice was for 298 Broadway on the property owned by Arthur F. May of Los Angeles. The building would have 4,034 square feet instead of the two thousand, thirty square feet in the present building. The ground breaking ceremony was planned but had to be delayed because the original architect's plans placed the building at the property

---

106. South Coast News. Jan. 10, 1941

POST OFFICE—LAGUNA BEACH 1390

PO on Broadway

line, and therefore a variance was needed. Because of necessary hearings the ceremony would be delayed for about two weeks.[107]

The building was completed and remains there today. R.V. Mead of Los Angeles was the General Contractor *"It was our privilege to build the post Office."* Public Lumber, 860 South Coast Blvd., supplied the lumber and building materials. The lighting was done by Bowles Electric, and *"The new P.O. is equipped with genuine, original 'Plumbing by Chris Valente'."*[108]

When Mrs. Ada Purpus became postmaster in 1934, there were four regular clerks and one substitute. By 1941, there were fourteen employees. They were L.F. Walden, assistant postmaster; Miss Harriet Boulanger, clerk; Walter Daschner, Irven Couse, William Laird and John Marriner,

107. South Coast News. April 15, 1941
108. South Coast News. Aug. 15, 1941

Nick Isch, unknown, Ada Purpus, Brayton Norton at opening of Braodway PO

clerks; Lloyd Babcock, John Heisy, Orville Goodrich, Bruce LePage and George Rickard, carriers; Harold Oelke, Edward Clair and Robert Kellogg, substitute clerk-carriers.[109]

For the grand opening a community breakfast was planned, with Tom Hosmer acting as chairman of the event. Sam Dawson would be the master of ceremonies, and Carolyn Weber was chairman of music and entertainment.[110]

The streets started filling at eight in the morning with Lagunatics who sang and enjoyed breakfast while listening to speeches. The new building provided double the floor space of the old post office building on Laguna Avenue.

John Nicholas Isch was acknowledged for getting the name of Laguna Beach officially recognized. Brayton Norton was there, and Mary Briggs, postmistress in Los Angeles was a special guest. Al Fanning, of Cottage City, said that they

109. South Coast News. March 14, 1941
110. South Coast News. Aug. 12, 1941

could use the empty lot he owned next to the new post office, Mrs. Harry Gordon Martin of the Episcopal Church said they would be happy to serve breakfast, Joe Jahraus offered to haul over the tables and chairs, and Tommy Swanson would provide the loud speaker. Tickets were put on sale at all of the drug stores.[111]

It is hard to picture a happier Laguna than on that day in August when the new post office building opened on Broadway. There was a huge public breakfast and celebration galore. *"Laguna dunked doughnuts this morning, dedicated a post office, heard words of praise spoken for the good things Ada Pupus, postmaster, has done for the community, and then went to work satisfied because long years of waiting for the postal building have ended."*[112]

The big move into the new building was set for Saturday noon at the close of business, and the new post office would be open on Monday morning. The biggest hitch seemed to be that there were all new box windows, with new, changed numbers. Many people had used the same number for years but now had to memorize a different one. Patrons were asked to please notify publishers and correspondents of the change of box number. The magazines, newspapers and periodicals were piling up.[113]

111. Laguna Beach Post. Aug.8, 1941
112. Los Angeles Times. Aug.16, 1941
113. South Coast News. Sept. 21, 1941

Post Office Box Doors.
Ken Lauher donation.
Photo: Johanna Ellis

When the Laguna Ave. post office building was no longer used, these box doors were removed and stored in a garage and eventually ended up with Dixie Larivee, who left them in the care of Ken Lauher, owner of Ken's Jewelry on Forest Ave. He has stored them and kept them safe for years, and has generously shared them for the post office history.

World War two was on the horizon, and Mrs. Ada Purpus took on the double duty of heading the local USO in Laguna during the war. When she retired as postmaster in May of 1945 she said that they had entertained 87,000 service men and women during 1944 alone.[114] Mrs. Purpus was truly active in Laguna for many years. She had come to Laguna in 1921, with her husband Roy. She at one time or another was President of the Chamber of Commerce, head of the local USO during the war, President of the Professional Woman's Club, President of the Woman's Club, member of the D.A.R., the Eastern Star, past President of the Ebell Club, Los Angeles, and a member of the Presbyterian Church.[115]

There is at least one tale of romance that came from delivering mail. Charles Masters had at one time delivered mail to the Maharaja and Maharanee of Indore in their palatial home in Laguna Beach at 758 Manzanita (now the Annelies School) It was reported that the Maharaja had an annual income of $70 million. The royal couple had divorced in 1943. Charles Masters was honorably discharged from the Coast Guard in 1943, and he and the Maharanee eloped to Las Vegas Nevada in 1945.[116]

Baird Coffin, local attorney, took over as postmaster April 30, 1945.[117] As the country and Laguna returned to normalcy after the end of the war, Mr. Coffin was pleased to

114. South Coast News. May 10, 1945
115. South Coast News. Dec. 2, 1954
116. Argus newspaper. Feb. 2, 1945
117. Official Post Office Records, National Archives

announce that there would once again be an afternoon mail delivery starting in September 1946. The lack of manpower had made it necessary to stop the twice-daily deliveries.[118] Yes, twice daily deliveries.

In 1947, mounted delivery service was being started in many of Laguna's more distant addresses in Laguna. All of Bluebird Canyon plus Temple Hills north of Thalia St. were gaining delivery, even though the streets that ran off of those main roads would have to group their mailboxes at the entrance of their street. For instance residents of Coast View Drive would have to put their boxes on the north side of the road, just beyond the *"not a through street"* sign. It was recommended that the residents of each of these streets get together and install one standard to hold all of the boxes.[119]

"Post Office on Wheels" was started in Laguna in 1948. Buses were converted to rolling post offices and were equipped to handle all the business at regular stops. They were designed to speed up pickup and delivery.[120] This did bring about an issue that caused no little static. To make space for the large bus to pull up twice daily, the two diagonal parking places in front of the building on Broadway were eliminated. Parking spaces have always been an issue in Laguna. Once again parking problems in front of the post office! To the complaints Police Chief Bachman said *"It's the best place to put it. It was already planned to eliminate one of the spaces because cars were being backed into pedestrian traffic at the corner and it was becoming more hazardous daily."*[121]

Additionally, more door-to-door mail delivery was to be added including the 500 blocks of Poplar, Linden and Center Streets, 300 block of Harold Drive, 600 block Pearl

---

118. South Coast News. Sept. 15, 1946
119. South Coast News. Sept. 23, 1947
120. South Coast News. Feb. 12, 1948
121. South Coast News. Aug. 24, 1948

St. and Palmer Place. Curb delivery was to start for residents on Emerald Terrace to the top of Ledroit and on Circle way between Cliff and Crescent Bay Drives.[122]

Post-war growth was progressing in Laguna with the addition of even more residents. Again in 1949, Postmaster Coffin had to add even more routes. Service was being extended to new neighborhoods and many that had received only car deliveries would in the future have door-to-door delivery. The list of extensions was long. This new addition would require the addition of two additional routes, making eleven in all. Before the war there had been only five routes in Laguna.[123]

---

122. South Coast News. April 6, 1948
123. South Coast News. May 19, 1949

Baird Coffin, left, greets new postmaster Walter E Parke at Broadway Post Office.
Credit: LB Historical Society

Due to all the added routes and home delivery, less room was needed for post office boxes in the building. Therefore, in 1952 the post office on Broadway was eliminating a whole section of boxes in the lobby, resulting in expanded work space for the postal employees.[124]

Baird Coffin resigned as postmaster in 1953, and the new postmaster was Walter E. Parke. Notice was received from Congressman Utt that the designation would be official May 14, 1953. The Parke family moved to Laguna in 1946, and as he was an accountant, served as a director and treasurer of the Laguna Beach Art Association, and also as an auditor for the Festival of Arts.[125]

Baird Coffin planned to stay in Laguna and was associating himself with the law firm of Osborne, Soloman and Fitts. He was Past President of the Chamber of Commerce, Past President of the Orange County Postmasters' Association and was at that time president of the Festival of Arts Association, treasurer at St. Mary's Episcopal Church and a Scout Leader of Boy Scouts of America.[126]

124. Laguna Beach Post. Feb. 13, 1952
125. South Coast News. April 21, 1953
126. South Coast News. April 21, 1953

The Post Office and the City Council were making front-page headlines in the two local newspapers in September of 1955. Usually the post office department dealt with private owners of land who built buildings that the post office leased, typically for ten years. At the heart of this new controversy was a bit of recently purchased city - owned land just past City Hall, where Forest Avenue ends and the Canyon Road begins, described as "bounded by Forest Avenue, the flood control channel and the Edison transformer station just north of City Hall, a matter of 8,376 square feet,"[127] Yes, even then they called it the Village Entrance. The town had known for at least two years that the building on Broadway was just too small for the growing population.

A larger post office was needed and to fill that need the real estate section of the Post Office Department proposed that a new post office be built on that piece of property. The problem was the way in which they carried out that attempt. The agent met only with city manager Ben Mead and the three city councilmen who were in town, Ben Sorrells, William Bachman, and Louis Zitnik. They worked out the proposal that was to be signed at that next Monday's City Council meeting.

Mayor Frank Wharton and Councilwoman Lyttle Rankin had both been out of town on vacation and learned of it only the day before the Council meeting. On the City Council agenda it appeared under "*New Business,*" and was listed simply as "*Consider agreement to lease city land.*"[128] City attorney Jack Rimel, who drew up the proposed lease said he received instruction to do so only the day before.[129]

---

127. Laguna Beach Post. . Sept. 15, 1955
128. Laguna Beach Post. Sept. 15, 1955
129. South Coast News. Sept.13,1955

Sherman Paddock, writing for the South Coast News, said that following the City Council meeting Sorrells, Bachman and Zitnik, were called into the City Clerk's office *"and subjected to a sharp grilling by three members of the press, representatives of the South Coast News, the Los Angeles Times and the Santa Ana Register."*[130] When called on the carpet they all replied that the post office agent *"had requested that everything having to do with the project be kept secret from the public, on the theory that if the news got around, and attempts to lease the city property failed, lease prices on other possible sites might be raised."*[131] Congressman Utt had not been told, nor had the Planning Commission nor the Chamber of Commerce. The Post Office Department did their best to keep everyone in the dark.

Mayor Wharton said if a building were put there that *"a 3-way traffic signal or a traffic officer would undoubtedly be required."*[132]

An editorial in the Laguna News Post said *"First look-out of city planners is the flow of traffic in their city, and the prevention, by planning with the future in mind, any possibility of traffic congestion. For this reason alone, in our opinion, local planners should recommend against a post office placed at the very mouth of a road which even now poses traffic congestion problems."*[133]

All this concern was even before the Santa Ana Freeway had been extended down to Irvine. They were all aware of the added traffic and problems that freeway would cause Laguna in the future, and as a result decided to postpone a decision until the Planning Commission could review the project, which they did in an emergency session, deciding against the project.

130. South Coast News. Sept. 13, 1955
131. South Coast News. Sept. 13, 1955
132. South Coast News. Sept. 16, 1955
133. Laguna Beach Post. Sept 15, 1955

"As no off-street parking is provided at the contemplated site, single and double parking along the easterly side of Laguna Canyon Road with its consequent invitation to illegal sweeping U turns into westbound road traffic, and single and double parking on the westerly side of the road with consequent pedestrian traffic across this wide intersection would create a traffic hazard beyond belief." [134] The City Council unanimously voted against the placement of a post office at that site.

What to put at the Village Entrance is not a new issue in Laguna's history.

The volume of mail continued to grow. In January of 1956, it was reported that the Christmas rush at the post office had resulted in the handling of one and a half million pieces of mail. This was done with the regular force of thirty-seven that was augmented by twenty-three Christmas assistants.[135]

New PM Eugene White Oct.1961. 570 Glenneyre St. Credit: LB Historical Society

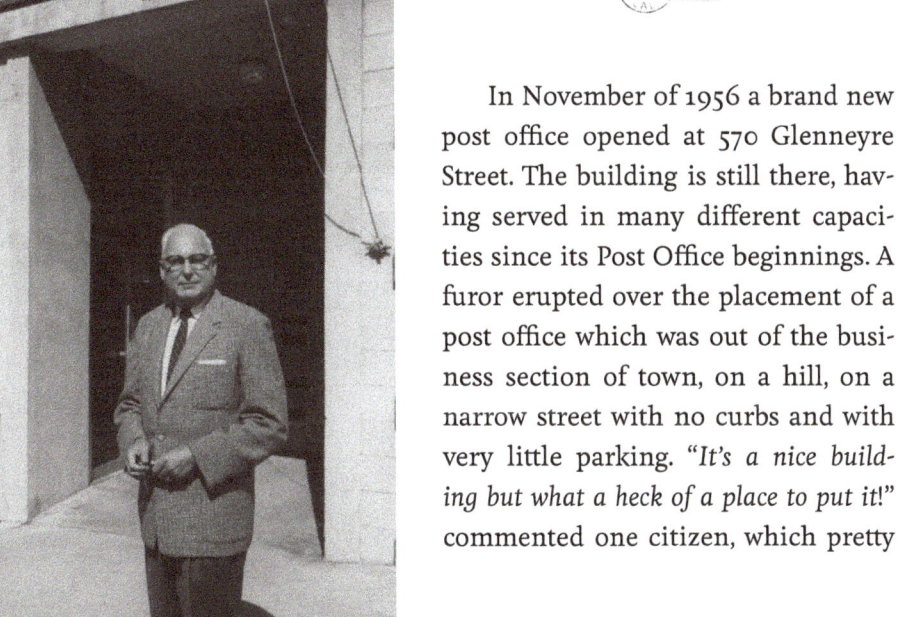

In November of 1956 a brand new post office opened at 570 Glenneyre Street. The building is still there, having served in many different capacities since its Post Office beginnings. A furor erupted over the placement of a post office which was out of the business section of town, on a hill, on a narrow street with no curbs and with very little parking. "*It's a nice building but what a heck of a place to put it!*" commented one citizen, which pretty

134. South Coast News. Sept. 23, 1955
135. South Coast News. Jan. 10, 1956

much summed up the reaction to the new building. A prominent ambulance owner wryly commented *"It's going to be a money-making proposition for me. I've seen two or three people almost get hit in the last ten minutes."*[136]

The City Council was quick to let it be known that they had nothing to do with the site selection - they heard of it only after the decision was made. Public safety was their big concern. Citizens had come forth with many suggestions of how to make it safer - put a cross- walk mid-block on Glenneyre, (that would surely lead to pedestrians being hit,) install a traffic light at the corner of Legion (that would back the traffic up all the way to Corona del Mar,) install sidewalks (that would cost more than the building itself and involve the moving of expensive buildings.) [137] Both City Manager Jay Mercer and Police Chief Victor Stewart emphasized that the problem was without a solution.

How often has a Post Office site been so inappropriate that a City Council passed a resolution condemning the location *as "detrimental to the health, welfare, and safety of the people"*? It happened in Laguna.[138]

"There is no solution to safety in that area" Mercer said, *"anything we could do just creates another hazard."*[139] The mental picture of elderly patrons having to walk up that steep hill to mail a package was mindful of the letter Henry Weeks had written years before.

How could this happen? A letter written by Verne Scoggins, director of the Post Office Department's San Francisco Regional Office, threw some light on the decision. *"The Glenneyre Street site was chosen because it was the best proposal to be submitted. There had been two sites suggested, the oth-*

---

136. South Coast News. Nov. 16, 1956
137. South Coast News. Nov. 23, 1956
138. South Coast News. Dec. 7, 1956
139. South Coast News. Dec. 7, 1956

er being on the south side of Second Street between Forest and Mermaid. That one was rejected because it did not offer accessibility for larger mail vehicles, it faced a narrow street with congested parking, and it backed onto a narrow one-way alley, and the traffic moves in the direction opposite to that which would offer the most convenient way of dispatching mail. The rent was in excess of that offered for the Glenneyre St. place. The fact that the Broadway location lease expired on Nov. 7 was also a factor."[140]

Postmaster Parke blamed the public outcry in opposition to the Laguna Canyon site for making it virtually impossible to find a site in the center of town."[141] The land and the new building were owned by Gwen N. Olander and others of Witchita Kansas, it involved a fifteen-year lease for the post office, and the transaction had been handled by the John Gilbert Realty.

There was another episode involving the unused old post office on Broadway. Just as the Isch post office appeared in scenes for a movie, the Broadway building was once again used as a post office - this occurred in 1957, when the abandoned building was used for exterior scenes in a movie titled *"Back From the Dead"* starring Peggie Castle, Arthur Franz, Marsha Hunt and Don Haggert. Several locations in Laguna were used in the movie. Trying to film on Broadway was a trying experience for the director Charles Marquis Warren. There were some barricades set up which local Lagunans completely ignored. The scene was set and cameras were ready to roll—wait, *"Move that gentleman in the blue shirt."* - Cut. Elmer Brown pedaled through the scene - Cut. Touch up powder applied on the actresses and just in time for the Laguna Ready-Mix truck to drive through - Cut. Carl Schramm drove by in his station wagon on his way to open his paint store -Cut. A man from Acord's Market tiptoed through - Cut. The entire membership of the Multiple

---

140.   South Coast News. Nov.27, 1956

141.   South Coast News. Nov.27, 1956

Listing Division of the Realty Board drove through, smiling - Cut. More scenes were planned at Victor Hugo's, Paradise Point, the beach, and Ocean Way.[142] Of particular interest were the scenes filmed around a house at 2192 Ocean Way, and some exterior scenes at the Ark House on Moss Street, both houses being gems of Laguna architecture and charm. Film critic Edwin Schallert said of the movie *"Another evidence of the supernatural influence in the cinema is the Charles Marquis Warren feature 'Back From the Dead,' which the producer-director-writer regards as offbeat for himself. It contains the idea of a dead person returning to gain possession of someone who is living."*[143] It would be difficult to recommend this movie, but the chance to see 1950s Laguna on screen is a little tempting.

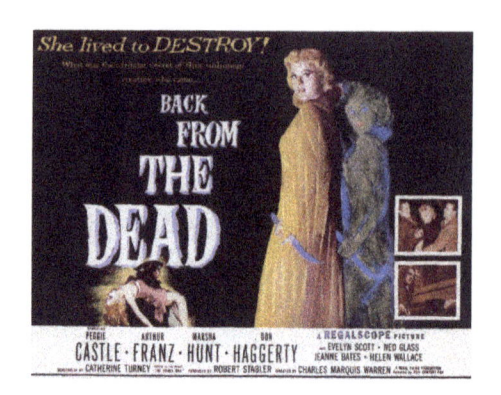

By November a new idea was being talked about around town - to put a "classified station" somewhere in an already existing business down in the main, flat part of town.

Postal inspector Short, way off in Los Angeles and unaware of local issues, said it might be a possibility, although he *"hadn't received one letter of dissatisfaction about the new post office."*

He had, however, heard from other people about the objections, and added *"the people will get used to the location, and I expect the business area will be growing in that direction"* indicating that it may be the business center in the future. Really? In explaining more about the classified station idea, he said that it was not technically a sub-station, but would be a part of some other business house. Store owners in good loca-

142. Laguna Beach Post. April 18, 1957
143. Los Angeles Times. April 12, 1957

Rubaiyat Book Shop Auxiliary PO. 332 Forest Ave. Credit: LB Historical Society

tions could contract with the post office to sell stamps, take in mail, parcel post etc. He said it would bring people in to a store and that would help the business.

Postal District Operations Manager Posey Christenberry, whose office was in San Diego, said that he would go along with any plan to help the conditions in Laguna. He said postmaster Walter Parke had forwarded to him one request from a businessman to have a classified station. He pointed out that regulations require stations to be at least one mile distant from the post office, and in this case it was only seven-tenths of a mile, but he added that there had been times in the past when that rule could be over-ridden. Previously, postmaster Parke had said he would not be in favor of having an auxiliary station here.

Laguna did get its auxiliary post office – it was in the Rubiayat Book Store at 268 Forest Avenue, owned by Mr. and Mrs. Carl Gilbert. It opened March of 1957, but three months later Gilbert was informed by postmaster Parke that the contract would not be renewed because it wasn't generating enough income to justify the $4,800 allowed. The citizens of Laguna rebelled and started petitions – there were eight businesses in town where one could go to sign. It worked, and the auxiliary station stayed open. Congressman Utt interceded and was able to get the decision over-ruled. Those 800 signatures certainly helped.[144]

The timing couldn't have been better – orders had come down from Washington to postmaster Parke that hours were going to have to be curtailed. The post office would be closed on Saturdays with no deliveries on that day, and regular

144. South Coast News. June 23, 1959

Auxiliary PO. Santa Fe Trailways Bus Depot 219 Ocean Ave.

hours would be shortened. Twelve of the thirteen mail carriers stayed home on Saturday, and at least 16 of the 38 regular employees were temporarily laid off. More than 140 man hours were cut by the order.[145]

Another sub-station was opened in Boat Canyon on Feb. 9, 1959. It was in Byron's Gift Shop in the Boat Canyon Shopping Center, and Byron Butler was in charge according to Postmaster Parke. Hours were from 9 a.m. to 5:30 p.m. Monday through Friday, and from 9 a.m. to noon on Saturdays. It could handle just about any mailing needs except foreign parcel post.[146]

The Gilbert sub-station in the Rubiayat Bookstore, which had moved further up the street to 332 Forest Avenue, was dealt a blow when verbally informed by postmaster Parke that the contract was going elsewhere. Starting on July

145. South Coast News. April 16, 1957
146. Laguna Beach Post. . Jan. 29, 1959

1,1959, the sub-station would be in the Trailways bus depot at 219 Ocean Avenue. The newspaper contacted Mrs. Regina Reiner at the bus depot to see if that were true, and she confirmed that she had submitted a proposal and that the sub-station was moving to Ocean Avenue.[147]

The year 1961 sounded like it might mark the end of what the local newspaper described as "Weary climbs up the hill on Glenneyre Street and mad dashes back to illegally parked autos in order to avoid tickets."[148]

The Bank of America was building a new bank over on Ocean Ave. and the building they were in now, at the corner of the Highway and Forest Avenue, would soon be available, so Congressman Utt contacted Laguna officials with information that the Postal Department was negotiating for a portion of that building. Utt sent a copy of the letter to Mayor Jesse Riddle in which the Operations Director said "we are very much aware of the serious parking situation at the main Post Office..... It will help if city authorities will establish limited parking lanes in front of this building for postal patron parking."[149]

Mayor Riddle and City Manager Jay Mercer said they would cooperate in any way possible to provide sufficient parking. There were still another ten years on the lease on Glenneyre, so the plan was to keep it as the main center, and to use the Bank building for mailing, stamp purchases, and box pick-ups . It didn't happen.

The end of the year did bring one change—a new postmaster, Eugene T. White was appointed.[150] On December 19, 1961, he made the locals happy by announcing that a new

147. South Coast News. June 23, 1959
148. South Coast News. March 10, 1961
149. South Coast News. March 10, 1961
150. US official PO records, National Archives

Hazel Kellogg,
PM White,
Jesse Riddell, Mayor
April 1962.
Credit: LB Historical Society

Post Office building would be located downtown near a large parking lot and that it should open in the spring of 1962. That is exactly what happened.

"*Hill-climbing and traffic-dodging days will soon be over for Laguna Beach postal patrons.*" was the opening sentence of an article in the paper about the opening of a post office down near the central part of town. The irony was that it was going right back into 236 Laguna Avenue where it had been in the Yoch building when Brayton Norton had been postmaster! (The post office had been in that building from 1923 until 1941.) Metaphorically this is called travelling full circle. That building was then owned by Margaret L. McKnight of Beverly Hills and would be leased from her for ten years at an annual rental of $6,956. Once the building was remodeled the change would be made. The Glenneyre building would still be used but only as a receiving station, and it would be called the Main Office, while the 236 Laguna Avenue building would be called the Finance Station.[151]

151. Laguna News Post. Jan.26, 1962

Vic Stewart, Police Chief, Jesse Riddle, Mayor, Stu Avis, Chamber of Commerce, Charles Nelson, Finance Superintendent, Elmer Brown, Chamber of Commerce, Eugene White, Postmaster. Laguna Ave. 1962. Credit: LB Historical Society

And a worry of the past had been removed – in the intervening years Laguna Avenue had been leveled, graded, lowered and paved. No more cars drifting across the street and crashing into each other on wet, muddy roads. And the Post Office now had a street number, something that didn't exist until the 1930s.

In April of 1962, there appeared in the newspaper a photo taken in front of the newly opened Laguna Avenue Post Office. Nothing but smiles grace the faces of the men in the picture. They each proclaimed the reason for their smile.

Police Chief Victor Stewart because *"a traffic hazard will be lessened on Glenneyre at the old, hard-to-get-to post office."*

Mayor Jesse Riddle *"is jubilant because he and the council deplored the Glenneyre choice."*

Stu Avis and Elmer Brown because *"they are Chamber of Commerce men and they like everybody to be happy."*

Charles Nelson, Finance Superintendent of the post office because *"the P.O has contented the citizen at last."*

Postmaster Eugene White because *"everybody feels friendly towards the post office once more."* [152]

---

152. Laguna News Post. April 5, 1962.

On August of 1968, Don Rose was appointed postmaster after Eugene White had resigned.[153] In June of 1973, the disappointing old post office at 570 Glenneyre Street was finally closing after nearly seventeen years of service. "The phase-out of the old office has brought few complaints, according to Postmaster Don Rose."[154] A third postal window was opened at this time at the Laguna Avenue office.[155]

Don Rose, Postmaster, announced in 1974, that he was retiring after seven years of post office service. Rose was born in Kansas and after graduating from Kansas University he worked as a manger for Bloomingdales in New York for fourteen years. He moved to California in 1948, and to Laguna in 1960. He ran as a Democrat for Secretary of State on the ticket with Pat Brown and served ten years as the Los Angeles Democratic County Commissioner. In Laguna he was active in the Chamber of Commerce, Beautification Committee and supported parks, open spaces, trees, Village Laguna and the Greenbelt.[156]

153. PO official records, National Archives
154. Los Angeles Times. June 2, 1973
155. Los Angeles Times. June 2, 1973
156. Coastline Pilot. Oct.25,2002

SOUTH LAGUNA

As South Laguna was annexed by the City of Laguna Beach on Dec. 31, 1987, the story of the post office for that area should be included. The central part of South Laguna, tract 849, was originally part of the homestead of Leon W. Goff Sr.[157] Later it was owned by Blanche Dolph, and in 1926, Lewis Lasley purchased it from her for $225,000 and it was named Three Arches. This is not to be confused with what is today the gated community of Three Arch Bay, which was then known as the Hallam Cooley tract.[158]

An interesting fact about the gated residential area of Three Arch Bay is that Mr. Cooley's original plan for that property was to build a hotel along the cliff front.

In 1933, Lasley and others began the effort to get a post office for the small village. Posters went up in Dana Point and Laguna Beach announcing that applications for postmaster were being taken. C.B. Clark was gathering signatures from residents that week requesting that the post office be named "Three Arches."[159]

Locals felt it was *"an economic waste for this community of over 300 adults to have to travel six or seven miles round trip for their mail."*[160]

The South Coast Improvement Association held a meeting at La Casa del Camino in November of 1933, where Laguna Postmaster Brayton Norton attended as a guest and talked about the proposed new post office for Three Arches which had been pending for some time. He had no rea-

---

157. Homesteader map by Beryl Viebeck
158. South Coast News. Nov. 9, 1934
159. South Coast News. Jan. 13, 1933
160. South Coast News. Nov. 17, 1933

son why it was taking so long and that he had posted in the Laguna Beach post office the notice of the calling for the examination for applicants, for which two had applied.

Grace Powers was appointed as postmaster on Dec. 22, 1933, and in January of 1934, the Three Arches Post Office opened. Jack Lasley was the first box holder and Frank Barr received the first letter.[161] The building was on the north east corner of Second Ave., and the Highway in a building owned by the Powers.[162]

The address of where that building would be today is the large building on the north east corner of Second Ave. at 31642 Coast Highway.

The name of Three Arches was short-lived. "*Arches*" was used in other places and the name just added to public confusion. The proposal was to change the name to South Laguna, because *"within 10 years it would be part of Laguna."*[163] Also in order to make the post office pay it needed to serve a larger number of people.[164]

The name-change did occur and as of December 1, 1934, the name became South Laguna. The area serviced was also enlarged to include Aliso Vista, Coast Royal, Goff Island, and Three Arch Bay.[165]

161. South Coast News. Jan. 19, 1934
162. South Coast News. June 7, 1949
163. South Coast News. March 16, 1934
164. South Coast News. Nov. 9, 1934
165. South Coast News. Nov. 9, 1934

Harland Cox
Credit: LB Historical Society

President Portus of the local association recommended that *"a good new sign be made at the expense of the association, and presented to the postmaster."*[166]

On Oct. 15, 1942, Harland Cox was appointed the new postmaster of South Laguna.

Just as the post office location in Laguna had changed over the years, the same followed suit in South Laguna. In April of 1946, the Power's building, which had been built in 1934, was moved to south of Third Ave. to a lot owned by Harry Berry.

Not to skip a beat, *"the post office was moved – lock, stock and stamps – and while it jogged serenely along the highway, it received delivery on the late afternoon mail. Postmaster Harland*

---

166. South Coast News. Nov. 16, 1934

Cox remained true to the Pony Express tradition that the mail must go through. Without halting the progress of his moving P.O. he caught the sacks as they were tossed off the mail truck into his arms. By the time the South Laguna Post Office came to rest on its new site a block and a half away, the admiring citizens were walking up the gangplank to collect their late-afternoon post cards, newspapers and bills."[167] The physical location of that building today is 31726 Coast Highway.

Don Estep in front of PO at 31726 Coast Highway

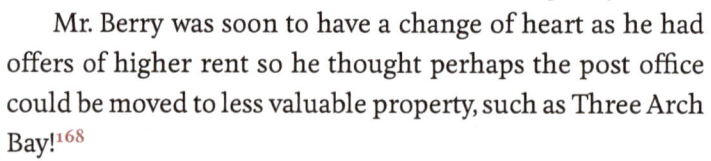

Mr. Berry was soon to have a change of heart as he had offers of higher rent so he thought perhaps the post office could be moved to less valuable property, such as Three Arch Bay![168]

Move it did, though not to Three Arch Bay. In the block between Third and Second Avenues there was a store that had been built by Augustus Thomas in 1927. Since 1945, it had been run by Mr. and Mrs. David G. Bowen. That building was about to be torn down in 1949, and Pharmacist Robert Jorden was about to erect a new concrete building reinforced to support a second story that would be added later.[169] He opened his *"Village Pharmacy"* in the northern side of the building and in June of 1949, the post office was moved into the southern side of the building at 31680 Coast Highway. Today that building still exists at 31678 Coast Highway. The room had more working space and 90 new boxes were added. Once again it was a smooth move – done after closing hours in the afternoon. *"Mr. Cox and his two assistants, Mrs.*

---

167. South Coast News.. April 2, 1946
168. South Coast News. Oct. l, 1946
169. South Coast News . Sept. 2, 1948

PO on right side of building

Frank Barr and Charles Linkey are courteous and efficient. They beam a welcome which makes such a prosaic thing as going after the mail a pleasant errand."[170]

Mail delivery service was introduced in January of 1950. As elsewhere, the home owner needed to have their house number displayed and a mail box that could be reached from an automobile. As in Laguna years before, there was a run on the sale of mail boxes. At this time no artists were giving advice on how to beautify mail boxes. There would be one delivery a day.[171]

In May of 1959, Harland Cox was granted the honor of being elected president of the State National League of Postmasters, an organization made up of about 400 mem-

---

170. South Coast News. June 2, 1949
171. South Coast News. Jan. 19, 1950

bers. The meeting was held in Forest Lake Resort, Cobb, Calif. At that time Cox was also Fire Chief of South Laguna's Volunteer Department.[172]

The second storey was eventually built onto the Jorden Building. In May of 1964, it was announced that *"South Laguna Post Office facilities have been completed at 31677 Virginia Way,"*[173] where it is still in use to this day.[174]

Harland Cox retired on Oct. 25, 1968.[175] That year also marks the end of the name of South Laguna Post Office. The Post Office Department announced that as of December 27, 1968, that the South Laguna Post Office would become a Classified Station of the Laguna Beach Post Office. Residents could go on using South Laguna, Calif. 92677 as their address, and they would still be provided with the same window and lock-box service.[176]

With the inclusion of the South Laguna Post Office into the Laguna Beach Post Office, that original triangular piece of Government homestead land, with three different names, was reunited in one way at least.

172. South Coast News. May 22, 1959
173. Los Angeles Times. May 17, 1964
174. Special thanks to Ann Christoph for defining newspaper descriptions of building locations. Photos are credited to the South Laguna Civic Association, the Jorden Family Collection.
175. Official Post Office Records, National Archives
176. Laguna News Post.. Nov. 27, 1968

New development in the surrounding areas had resulted in consolidation of the post offices of the area so that by Dec. 1968, Laguna Niguel, South Laguna, and Laguna Hills were designated "classified" branches of the Laguna Beach Post Office.[177]

David Rios was appointed postmaster of that entire area in June of 1974. He started his career as a letter carrier in Laguna. In 1971, he was appointed foreman of mails and in 1973, he was made acting superintendent of mails.[178] He announced that the post office was about to make some changes in how it functioned. *"Forwarding mail has always been a big operation. Previously it was handled by the carriers, but now it will be done by others, freeing the carriers for better delivery service. Bill Cunning will be in charge of mail processing and Grady Crowley will be manager of customer service, in charge of moving a million and a half pieces of mail a day."*[179] Around the early 1970s a carrier annex was used in Laguna Canyon – today's address is 2295 Laguna Canyon Road, located just about across the street from today's School of Art.

Jim Nordstrom at Laguna Canyon Building

177. News Post. Dec. 28, 1968
178. Los Angeles Times. Dec. 12, 1974
179. News Post. June 8, 1974

By December of 1974, construction had started on a new shopping complex in Laguna. It was on the site of the old Laguna Lumber on Forest Avenue, which had moved out into the canyon. When Joe Jahraus came home from France at the end of World War 1, he had "*a fistful of picture postcards*" showing architecture in France that he wanted emulated in Laguna. Jann Egasse was the architect for the building of the old Laguna Beach Lumber Co. office. The new $2.5 million dollar group of buildings was designed by Ib Christian Abel who said "*It was a challenge to create contemporary buildings and still keep the Norman feeling. We have done it with steeply slanted roofs, used brick, flagstone and timber.*"[180]

By June of 1975, work had begun on a new building on the Lumber Yard property to be leased by the Laguna Beach Post Office at 384 Forest Avenue.[181] It would cost $150,000 and it was hoped that it would be completed in August. It was anticipated that the move would be made from Laguna Avenue to Forest Avenue in September of 1975. There would be plenty of reserved parking for the public, where there was none on Laguna Avenue. It would still have six employees, three service windows, and the number of postal boxes would increase from the present 1,600 to 2,600.[182]

That marks 1975, as the year of finally getting a post office that could handle all possible needs of the future and there would be no more new buildings or moves in town. In the years ahead, though, there were changes that could not have been known then.

---

180. LA Times. Dec. 8, 1974
181. Conversation Dick Jahraus
182. Los Angeles Times. June 6, 1975

There were new housing developments in surrounding areas that were included into the Laguna Post Office system. New more efficient equipment was invented and there were cost-cutting advancements made. There are 2,700 mail boxes and an average of 4 employees that work in that building on Forest Ave. Today, 2018, the building is no longer the Laguna Beach Post Office, it is called Playa Station. The mail delivered to residents is dispensed from Aliso Viejo and, alas, a letter mailed from Laguna carries the postmark of Santa Ana, California.

Curiously – as in some weird historical time warp, the postmark for Laguna Beach once again does not match the name of the town.

SOME WHO SERVED

Special Thanks to Butch Chadick for name identification.

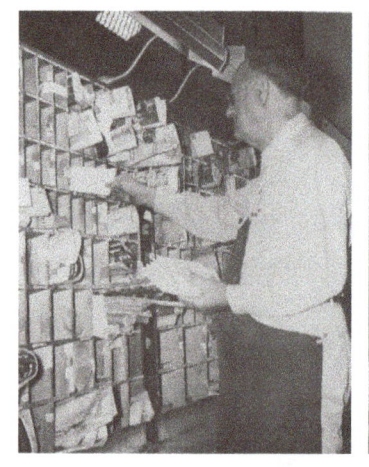

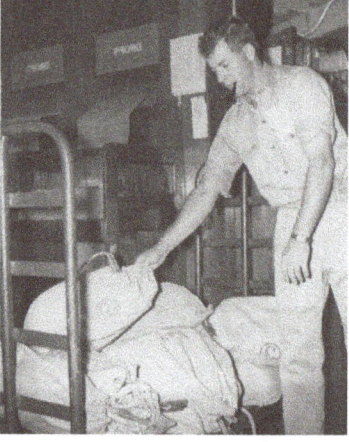

Far Left: Daniel Hankey

Left: Forrest Johnson

Mr. Chavez PO

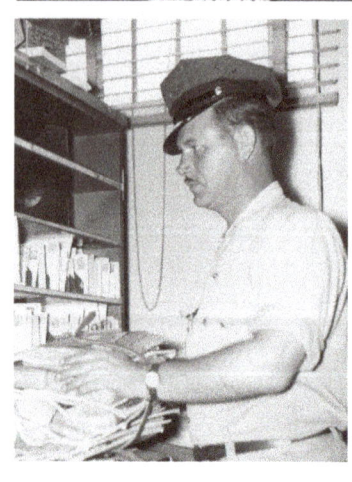

Far Left: Marlin Iglebart
10-2-58

Left: James Quam

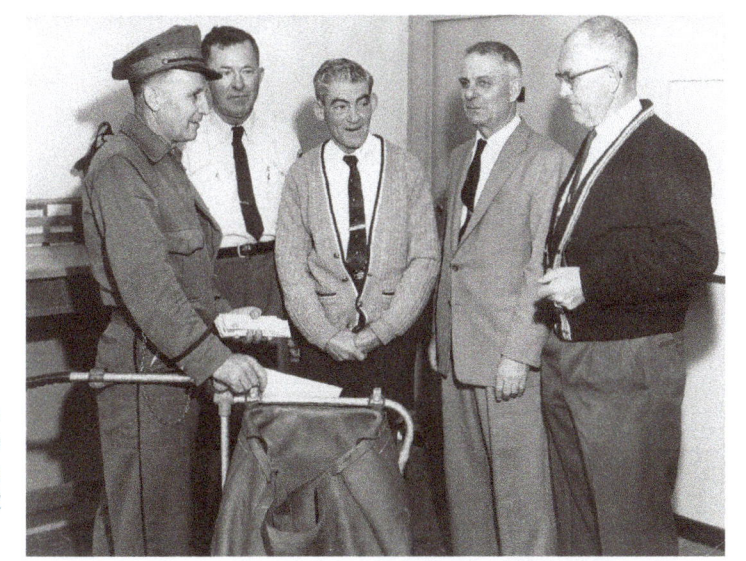

John Heisey, Bruce La Page, Eddie Clair, Irwin Couse, Bob Kellogg
April 1962

PM White, Jan.1962

2018 reunion of letter carrierrs. Ron Musical, Denny Deneff, Dave Rios, Butch Chadick, Bud Pool and front Gregg Stewart.
Photo courtesty of Eileen Acord Chadick

JANE JANZ

SOURCES: BOOKS

Brigandi, Phil. "Orange County Place Names A to Z" Sunbelt Publications. 2006

Cleland, Robert Glass. "From Wilderness to Empire" Alfred A. Knopf. 1944

Dumke, Glenn S. "The Boom of the Eighties" Huntington Library. 1944. Sixth Printing. 1991

Fisher, MFK. "To Begin Again." Pantheon 1992

Frickstad, Walter N. "A Century of California Post Offices." A Philatelic Research Society Publication. 1955

Friis, Leo J. "Orange County Through Four Centuries." Pioneer Press. 1965

Gudde, Erwin G. "California Place Names." University of California Press. Third Edition, 1969. Second Printing, 1974

Meadows, Don. "Historic Place Names in Orange County." Paisano Press. 1966

Newmark, Harris. "Sixty Years in Southern California 1853-1913." Zeitlin & VerBrugge. 1979

Patterson, Tom. "A Colony for California" Riverside's First Hundred Years. Press-Enterprise Company. 1971

Pleasants, Mrs. J.E. "History of Orange County California. Vol.3. J.R Finnell & Sons. 1931

Salley, H.E. "History of California Post Offices" Second Edition 1849-1990. 1991 The Depot (copyright) Number 439 of 500 copies.

Sleeper, Jim . "Jim Sleeper's 2nd Orange County Almanac." Ocusa Press. 1974

Starr, Kevin. "California." 2005 Modern Library Edition. 2005

Thurston, J.S. "Laguna Beach of Early Days." Murray and Gee, Culver City, Ca. 1947

Van Dyke, Theodore S. "Millionaires of a Day." Fords, Howard, & Hulbert. 1890

Woolsey, Ronald C. "Will Thrall and the San Gabriels – A Man to Match the Mountains." San Diego Sunbelt Publications. 2004.

Yoch, James J. "Landscaping the American Dream." A Ngaere Macray Book. Harry N. Abrams. New York. 1989